invite
PRESS

Dr. Brunson's *God is For You* is like a close friend sharing a secret earned from a life poured out for the gospel. With a skilled hand, Brunson reminds us that wisdom is a process. God does not open our head and pour in wisdom all at once. Godly wisdom - doing what reflects the purpose of God for our lives - humbles us and causes us to trust God for every decision in life. Through the life-tested and sure touch of a preacher five decades in the making, Brunson brings us back time and again to Solomon's admonition: in all your getting, get wisdom. Then speaking from that same wisdom, Brunson leaves us with this much-needed encouragement: "nothing passes into our life that does not first come under the vigilant eye of God the Father, through the nail-scarred hands of Jesus, and past the sentinel safeguard of the Holy Spirit."

—**Charles Martin**, *New York Times* bestselling author

In his must-have, eclectic, refreshing and renewing work, *God is For You,* Dr. Mac Brunson combines relatable contemporary illustrations, biblical insights and personal experiences to provide relevant encouragement for timeless generations. This is not a work produced by an unaware armchair theologian or one unacquainted with the vicissitudes of life. Readers are challenged by trustworthy lessons from a voice strengthened by faith and soothed by the promises of our faithful God—even in dark times. Let the reader with ears to hear read and hear the voice of God in these pages.

—**Robert Smith, Jr.**, Charles T. Carter Baptist Chair of Divinity, Beeson Divinity School, Samford University

This book is the embodiment on paper of Mac Brunson: warmhearted, genial, amiable, passionate, and biblical. With a practiced pastoral kindness, he embraces his own crisis on the front porch of this book and then affectionately counsels you with a kindhearted sensitivity that stands alongside the reader in solidarity rather than above the reader in superiority. These pages take you by the hand and lead you through your crisis rather than standing at a distance giving advice. Every page evokes the present power of past biblical persons – a characteristic of this practiced pastor who looks at life as it really is without blinking. The book generously grants grace.

— **Joel C. Gregory**, Holder of the George W. Truett Endowed Chair of Preaching, Baylor's Truett Seminary

This book uplifted my spirit. With the deft use of biblical insights and illustrations, Mac Brunson reminds us that God gives wisdom to those who truly seek it. Read this book and then pass it along to others to encourage them to believe that God is faithful to His people in the day of trouble.

—**Erwin Lutzer**, Pastor Emeritus, The Moody Church, Chicago, Illinois

Knowledge abounds. Wisdom is in short supply. Here is an excellent book on wisdom by Mac Brunson, one of the wisest pastors I know. Though we need wisdom every day in life, life's crises have a way of going deeper than our wisdom can handle well. At such times, we need to let our bucket down deep in God's wisdom. This solidly biblical and wonderfully practical book is succinct, clear, and readable. Once I started reading it, I could hardly put it down. Don't miss this gem—it's worth its weight in gold.

—**David L. Allen**, Distinguished Professor of Practical Theology, Dean of the Adrian Rogers Center for Biblical Preaching, Mid-America Baptist Theological Seminary

This is the book all of us need not just in crisis but in preparation for the inevitable, unexpected trials life dishes up. When my own life unexpectedly imploded leaving me a sudden widow and single mom to seven, Mac Brunson's sound teaching was a weekly lifeline as I navigated the overwhelm of crushing pain and countless decisions. In *God Is for You*, Mac brings his signature storytelling, pastor's heart, and Biblical theology through the life of Moses to give us principles of godly wisdom. If you've viewed godly wisdom as too obscure to attain, this book delivers practical truth from scripture every one of us can apply.

—**Lisa Appelo**, author of *Life Can Be Good Again: Putting Your World Back Together After It All Falls Apart*

As believers, we are told to "acquire wisdom above all." Thankfully for us, Mac Brunson's *God is For You* gives us rich insights on how to grow in wisdom, using Bible characters as examples. Drawing lessons from their experiences, he presents clear illustrations of what godly wisdom is. Each chapter ends with thoughtful questions, helping the reader work through these Biblical truths. If you are seeking wisdom, this exceptional book is for you!

—**Susie Hawkins**, ministry wife, author, Bible teacher

It's one thing to know that we can trust the wisdom of God, but how to access that wisdom and the faith to trust God's wisdom is quite another. Mac Brunson has written a powerful resource that equips us to be able to access the perfect wisdom of God, while reminding us that trusting our own wisdom is flawed. Wisdom is so lacking, not just in the world, but too many times in the church. This book is a must-read for all who truly seek wisdom.

—**Rick Burgess**, radio host, speaker, and Director of
TheManChurch.com

What a combination: *rare candor and real crises*. Yes, we all have crises in life, yet we seldom experience candor about what I consider the most painful word in existence – betrayal. Personally, I've experienced gut wrenching betrayal. However, here in the Olympic Theater. Mac Brunson wins the gold for his focus on wisdom and how we can trust God's wisdom through our crises. Because we all desperately need wisdom as we run the unpredictable race of life, this is a book we all need.

—**Jane Hunt**, Founder, CSO (Chief Servant Officer), Hope for the Heart
and The Hope Center. Author of *Counseling Through Your Bible Handbook*
and *How to Forgive When You Don't Feel Like It*

Mac Brunson shares a walked-in, fought for wisdom that only true experience and hardship can teach.

—**Rebekah Hannah**, Executive Director, Anchored Hope

Brunson offers wise biblical guidance to point his readers toward faithful worship, trust, and obedience. I am happy to recommend *God Is for You*.

—**David S. Dockery**, President, Southwestern Baptist
Theological Seminary

God Is for You

MAC BRUNSON

God Is for You

Learning to Trust God's Wisdom through Life's Crises

invite
PRESS

Plano, Texas

Dedication

To the Congregation of God's People
Valleydale Church
You have been to me the wisdom of God and the love of Jesus Christ

God Is for You
Copyright 2023 by Mac Brunson

This book is printed on acid-free, elemental chlorine-free paper.

ISBN Paperback 9781953495938; eBook 9781953495945

Scripture references are taken from the (NASB®) New American Standard Bible®, Copyright © 1960, 1971, 1977, 1995, 2020 by The Lockman Foundation. Used by permission. All rights reserved. lockman.org.

Scripture references marked ESV are taken from The Holy Bible, English Standard Version® (ESV®) © 2001 by Crossway, a publishing ministry of Good News Publishers. All rights reserved.

Scripture references marked KJV are taken from the King James Version of the Bible. Rights in the Authorized (King James) Version of the Bible are vested in the Crown Rights in the Authorized (King James) Version of the Bible are administered in the United Kingdom by the Crown's patentee, Cambridge University Press.

23 24 25 26 27 28 29 30 31 32 —10 9 8 7 6 5 4 3 2 1

MANUFACTURED in the UNITED STATES of AMERICA

Contents

Foreword
Psalm 42

Some days are doozies. Some days are for sure harder than others. Nobody knows that better than King David. I could take you to several of the Psalms he wrote and show you a man with a broken heart, a man with a confused mind, a man with a disordered world, a man who is living through a dark night of the soul. A specific Psalm that comes to mind when I'm in one of those upside-down moments is Psalm 42. The Psalm starts like this,

> As a deer pants for flowing streams,
> so pants my soul for you, O God.
> My soul thirsts for God,
> for the living God.
> When shall I come and appear before God?

Here's something that you would know about me if you spent five minutes with me - I like to hunt. That might be an understatement, but I have for sure spent a lot of time in the woods in my life. That means that I've spent a lot of time observing deer in my life. That makes me a bit of an expert on this passage. Deer don't just pant in their free time. Deer only pant in one of three situations. First, they pant when they are chasing something - usually a buck chasing a doe. Second, they pant when they are fighting which is usually bucks fighting over does as well. Third, they pant when they are being hunted and they are running for their lives from someone like me. That is more than likely what David is writing about in this text. The deer is running and is at the brink of exhaustion and is desperate for a drink of water, but it can't stop because it's afraid for its life. Have you ever been there? Have you ever found yourself desperate for hope and help from God? Are you there right now? Maybe there's a medical diagnosis that you have no clue how to face. Maybe there's a family member that's running hard in the wrong direction and ruining their life. Maybe your spouse wants out. Maybe your boss just let you know you need to clean out your office.

We all face moments that feel overwhelming and confusing. It's a very real part of life. Wisdom is just a word until you're desperate for help just like the deer in Psalm 42. You don't need someone to tell you what you did wrong. You need wisdom. You need to know how to navigate the situation that fills the windshield of your life. Like David, you need God. Did you know that one of that character traits of God is that He is omnisapient? I am sure that that last sentence didn't stir your affections for God or help you with the thing you're walking through, but that's because I used the word "omnisapient" and not "all-wise." Omnisapient is a big word that means that God has all wisdom and is all-wise. God knows everything and He always knows what to do. That means that there is not a single moment in your life when God doesn't know exactly what is going on and what you need to do. That should give you some peace right now, no matter where you are or what's going on. God knows and has a plan. Maybe though, part of the tension in this moment is that you're afraid of God. I get that. I mean, if there is a God and He's in control of all things, what in the world is He doing? If He loves you and He's all-powerful, wouldn't He keep you out of this mess? I've been there and I've asked those same questions.

Here's the thing about being all wise, you know exactly the right thing to do which will lead things to the perfect place. God knows how to get you exactly where He wants you to be and where you need to be. He knows how to take things that seem really heavy and hard and perfectly work them to reveal His heart for you. If that's the case, then that means that the friction in those moments isn't that God is doing something or isn't doing something but that you and I are not God. I would for sure have scripted things differently in my story as I am sure you would for your life, but I'm not all-wise nor are you. God might have you in a place that hurts or feels confusing right now because He wants you to lean into Him and to trust Him. Here's what makes these moments so significant. It's not just that God is all-wise but He's also good. He loves you so much that He will direct your life towards Himself.

So, if God is all-wise, all good, and He's doing something, what do we do in those moments when life feels upside down? Where do we get the wisdom we so desperately need? I'm assuming that's why you picked up this book on Godly wisdom. Psalm 42 gives us three ways that we can find Godly wisdom. First, David points out in verse 4 that in that moment of desperation he remembered times he had in worship. Second, He tells us in verse 5 that he remembers the things that God has done. Finally, the whole Psalm acts as a reminder and way finder for believers throughout history as David shares his own story.

First, David encourages us to lean into worship when we need wisdom. Worship is war. In the Old Testament the worship leaders lead the people of Israel into battle. Worship is where the things rolling around in our head collide with the truth of God and His Word. When we are in a desperate place we desperately need to get before God, beside His people, and declare truth together.

One of the most desperate moments in my life came in 2021. The elders at my church had graciously given me a sabbatical and on that time off I went red stag hunting in the highlands of Scotland with two of my best friends, Lars Peterson and Brad Bowen. We all headed out on October 13th, but Brad never came back. He had a heart attack and died while hiking in the highlands on that hunt. I cannot even begin to describe the heartache, confusion, and desperate moments that ensued over the next few days, weeks, and months. Here's the wild thing that happened in my heart and mind. All I could think about was getting back to my church, to Eleven22. I wasn't thinking about preaching or getting home, I was consumed with wanting to worship with my faith family and get to the altar to pray and cry out to God.

God meets us in those moments of worship and stabilizes our hearts and minds with Himself. He gives us perspective. That doesn't just mean that He helps us see through the situations we are in, more importantly He helps us see Him. David later writes in Psalm 121,

> I lift up my eyes to the hills.
> From where does my help come?
> My help comes from the Lord,
> who made heaven and earth.

David wrote this Psalm as one of the Psalms of Ascent that the people of Israel would sing as they made their way up to the temple to worship. He wrote it to be a rhythm for them to remember in the moments when they needed help remembering that God is there. It was meant to be a reorientation to a disoriented people. That's us. Worship is supposed to do the same thing for us. What could be wiser than in a moment of panic to point you to the God who has all wisdom and is all wise? When it's hard and it hurts, you need a faith family to worship with.

The second place you will find wisdom is in the scriptures. David reflects on all of the things that God had done for Him and for Israel. He says he remembers Jordan, Mt. Hermon, and Mt. Mizar. These are key landmarks that point to the land of Israel. David is remembering the promises that God made to Abraham in Genesis. He's remembering how God protected Joseph and the children of Israel in Egypt. He remembers how God brought them out of bondage and through the Red Sea. He remembered how God led and provided for them in the wilderness for 40 years. He remembered how God led them through the Jordan river and into the Promised Land. He remembered how God went before them and helped them conquer the land. He remembered how God had worked and it gave him hope that God was still at work even in his desperate situation. David had learned to look back.

Often when you're hunting, and you shoot a deer it will run to get away from the threat and pain. As a hunter you have to follow what is known as "the blood trail" which is where the wound from the bullet or arrow bleeds out. Sometimes you lose the trail. You will see and follow drops of blood and then nothing. What I do is use toilet paper on the trees to mark where I have seen drops of blood so when I lose the trail I can look back and see where the deer had been going. Nothing is a better determiner of where the deer will go than where it has been. That is what David is doing, he's looking back at all the ways that God has protected and provided for His people. That history gives David hope for his present and his future.

That is exactly what reading the Bible does for you and me. As we read about Abraham, Isaac, Jacob, Joseph, Moses, David, Israel, the disciples, and the early church we see how faithful God has always been to His people. We also read His timeless words that are truth for us right now that we need to lean into and trust. Our all-wise God has spoken, and we can get the wisdom we so desperately need by reading and applying His words.

Here's the final source for wisdom, David shares his story with Israel and with us. That's exactly what Dr. Brunson has done in this book. He shares his story of being in a desperate place and needing wisdom and then unfolds for you and me how God met him and guided him through the crisis he found himself in. There's nothing like a good guide. When you have someone who knows the terrain and has spent time there before, they can help you not only navigate with ease but also can point out things that you might have missed otherwise. I'm so thankful for my friend Mac Brunson and his vulnerability in sharing his story but also that our good God walked him through that season so that he could do exactly what David did in Psalm 42 and guide us to our God who is all-wise.

My daddy used to tell me often as a kid, "Joby, if you're going to be dumb, you better be tough." Life has a way of making you tough. It has a way of placing you in moments that are beyond your comprehension. We have a way of wandering into some pretty lost situations.

God also has a way of using confusing things to change everything. Hear the heart of the Father who pleads with us to "Get wisdom, and whatever you get, get insight." If you will lean in and read this book, I know that it will guide you to the wisdom that you desperately need. And I pray more so that you will hear from the heart of the all-wise God who loves you and is with you even in the most desperate moments.

Joby Martin
Pastor of The Church of Eleven22 in Jacksonville, FL
Author of *If the Tomb is Empty* and *Anything is Possible*

Introduction

CRISIS. Just the word stirs up inexpressible emotions. No one expects them. By sheer definition, you never know the timing, place, make-up, or extent of a crisis. Mine hit at around seven o'clock one Monday morning in Jacksonville, Florida, in the back booth of a little greasy spoon where I loved to have breakfast. Just a few simple words set the crisis in motion, but they struck me like a ton of bricks. It was like Poe's raven showing up at the window of my heart, tapping and quipping, "Never more." This crisis would come back to my memory again and again, just like in "The Raven." No one else would have given those words that morning thought, but deep down in my soul I knew that it meant crisis. What I didn't know was how big the crisis was going to be. It would become the kind of crisis that would change the trajectory of my life forever.

The main aspect of a crisis is that you never know you are headed into one until you are in the midst of it. No one schedules a crisis. It would be great if we could schedule all crises on Thursday afternoons between three and five o'clock—at least that way we could be prepared—but they just never seem to work out that way. You simply never see them coming.

Health Crisis

I had just been through a physical crisis with my health. It too came out of the blue one Saturday while sitting at my desk. My head began to pound. It was a headache unlike any I had ever had before. Yet I decided to push through Sunday, caught a plane for Chesapeake, Virginia, where I was scheduled to preach in a pastors' conference. The plane ride seemed to intensify the headache. After I preached I went straight back to the hotel and crawled into bed. The next morning found me back on a plane for Jacksonville, but with a headache I can only describe as head crushing. To be honest, I don't remember getting off the plane, going to my car, driving to the doctor's office. I do remember pulling out every credit card in my pocket and walking to the doctor's receptionist and saying, "Here is every credit card I've got. My head is hurting so bad that I am going to lie here in front of this front desk until you get me back to the doctor." Let me tell you, that is the quickest way to get a doctor's appointment. I don't remember anything that happened after that until I looked up and saw my wife, Deb, standing beside me as I lay on an examining table.

It turned out I was suffering from a spontaneous spinal fluid leak. "Spontaneous" means they don't know what caused it. When this happens and you sit upright or stand up, your brain settles down with no fluid to suspend it. The memory of the pain is enough to run cold chills down my spine. My spinal fluid barely, and I mean scarcely, registered at all with a spinal tap. This issue had gone on for over a month before I received any kind of treatment. Thankfully, a great young doctor, who happened to be my chairman of the deacons, intervened in the diagnosis and treatment. After a simple but frightening procedure, I was miraculously well.

This was a medical storm that blew in out of nowhere, a crisis of such personal proportion that I thought I was going to die. Tragically, at the same exact time, my best friend from Southwestern Baptist Theological Seminary, Chip Roberson, lay dying with brain tumors. In spite of the severity of our situations, Chip and I both laughed in what turned out to be our last conversation together. We both had "brain" issues when most folks thought we had no brains at all.

Thinking back on that year, I actually recall being faced with multiple crises. My dad died quite unexpectedly, and then my mother died six months later. This spinal fluid medical crisis exploded on me, then my best friend passed away, all within eleven months. Little did I know that the crisis that would change my life was just ahead of me. What could be worse than the year in which I had experienced a medical emergency and lost my dad, mom, and best friend? Believe it or not, that year would turn out to be a cake walk in comparison to the personal, spiritual crisis that I was sailing into.

For nearly a year after the medical crisis, my doctor at Mayo repeatedly told me I needed to take some time off. "Just take a month at least off. I mean with no work at all, no cell phone, no preaching," he pleaded. Dr. Willis was a friend and a very active member of his church, Bethel Baptist in downtown Jacksonville. He eventually looked at me and said, "If you don't agree to take the time off, I'm going to talk to your deacons." I went home and told Deb that we were taking off for a month, doctor's orders. The lingering exhaustion from the spinal fluid leak and the fear of the headaches coming back were simply draining.

It took me about a week longer to truly follow orders. I preached on Sunday, flew to Texas, and spoke seven more times over the next seven days. Monday morning on a plane back to Jacksonville, Deb leaned over and looked at me with her huge brown eyes and said, "You are mine, and this is it. We are headed to the mountains, and you are not going to speak again for three weeks. Give me your cell phone." She meant business, and I knew exactly what to say: "Yes, Ma'am."

Personal Crisis

Three weeks in the mountains was just what the doctor ordered and what this preacher needed. Again, no one knows when crisis is coming until it hits. That first day back in the office after our mountain retreat, it hit with the intensity of a tsunami. You never quite know how to take betrayal. To try to grasp it, I read and reread the story of David. How do you handle your close friend betraying you? Psalm 55:12-14 resonated in my ears:

> For it is not an enemy who reproaches me,
> Then I could bear it;
> Nor is it one who hates me who has exalted himself against me,
> Then I could hide myself from him.
> But it is you, a man my equal,
> My companion and my familiar friend;
> We who had sweet fellowship together
> Walked in the house of God in the throng.

Ah, Ahithophel, the counselor of David whose counsel was as if one had inquired of the LORD (2 Samuel 16:23). Ahithophel turned on David to support Absalom's rebellion. Or what about Absalom, his own son, who would turn the hearts of the people away from his father, David? How did David face such hurt and betrayal?

I wondered how General George Washington felt when one of his excellent fighting generals turned out to be Benedict Arnold, the traitor. I thought, *how did the founding fathers feel when Aaron Burr attempted to build his own kingdom west of the Mississippi?* None of us could fathom what Christ went through, but in my circumstance, I certainly had come to a better understanding of how wickedly painful betrayal can be. My mind flew back to the breakfast in the restaurant when I knew that those specific words signaled a crisis coming. Now I knew—my first impression had been right: CRISIS.

Men who had been loyal, committed, trustworthy, and loving suddenly had became distant without explanation. These were friends in whom I had placed great confidence. Men to whom I had ministered, even in times of the death of their loved ones. Men who had turned toward me to pray with them when marriage issues became painful and tense. Men whom I had counseled and thrown my arms around to encourage. Men I had prayed with about the deepest issues of their lives. Men who suddenly treated me as if I had COVID, or leprosy, or worse. They now looked at me and never smiled. They barely spoke. They hardly made eye contact.

Spiritual Crisis

Then the meetings started, and they would come about every month. It began with a phone call from one of these men who asked me to meet with him. Then the other calls came from three men, men I thought would have stood by me through anything. Now they stood against me. The recommendation they offered me was to step aside and get out of the way of what they had plotted and planned. They offered me a much-diminished role in the very church that I had pastored for twelve years. In the midst of the crisis, all I could think was, *how in the world did I not see this coming?*

What had started out as a crisis at work had now escalated into a crisis in the ministry to which God had called me and now seeped into my own personal spiritual life. Where had I failed God? I knew I was a sinner, but come on, I wasn't Charlie Manson. Every day I would pray for the LORD to reveal to me the gross sin in my life that I might repent. Have you ever been there? "LORD if this is your punishment, tell me the infraction that was so disgusting that being betrayed, lied about, ostracized, and marginalized is the payment." It was difficult to believe that men I had trusted and who had trusted me could so insidiously, covertly, and furtively transform. Every meeting felt like an inquisition. There were no right answers. Believe me, I sought them.

This was no simple crisis. It was a crisis of a spiritual nature, and it was not small but of megalithic proportions. I was now at the end of my rope. Honestly, I was at the end of the extent of my wisdom. In fact, there was a crisis in my wisdom.

One morning Deb walked up the stairs at the house and came into my study. She came through the door holding her Bible. Over to my side she came and said, "God has given me a word for us." I was anxious to hear anything. I felt like such a failure. I had failed my family, my wife, the church, and God. All I could think was that I was so glad my dad was not here to see this. He had always been my hero and the wisest man I had ever known. He had little education, having only completed the eighth grade. He was born in 1922, lived through the dark days of the depression in the South, and, like many children, had to go to work to help support his family. I was actually the first to get an education in my family. I earned a doctorate of ministry from Southwestern and was working on a PhD from there as well. What would Dad say if he were here? What wisdom would he give me? I wanted to hear from someone, but, again, I was so grateful that he never saw me go through that crisis.

With all this on my heart, Deb pointed out a verse, and said, "This is it, Exodus 14:14," and she read it to me: "The LORD will fight for you while you keep silent." It was as if I had heard from on high. I guess I had. Be quiet. Stop all the whining and crying and all the defeatist scenarios going through your head: "My ministry is over. I will be shunned. No one will ever want me to fill a pulpit again, much less be a pastor." Spiritual battle is real, and I was as beat down as a man could get.

Wisdom in Crisis

There is a world of difference in experiencing a crisis in your wisdom, your thinking, or your judgment, and *Wisdom in Crisis*. What I needed was wisdom in the midst of my crisis, and not just any wisdom. When Deb walked out of my study, I began to pray and ask the LORD for a word, a passage from His word. Somehow, I went to Psalm 118:

> Give thanks to the LORD, for He is good;
> For His lovingkindness is everlasting.
> Oh let Israel say,
> "His lovingkindness is everlasting."
> Oh let the house of Aaron say,
> "His lovingkindness is everlasting."
> Oh let those who hear the LORD say,
> "His lovingkindness is everlasting."

From *my* distress I called upon the LORD;
The LORD answered me *and set me* in a large place (emphasis mine).

The phrase that jumped out at me was *my distress* in 118:5. The word in the Hebrew literally describes a narrow place that is increasingly getting tighter. It's the picture of a room where the walls are closing in on you.

That was me. That was the church. It was all closing in on me by someone else's design, and I was choking to death. I have never had a panic attack before but have counseled people who have. I stood on that precipice twice during this crisis. In both cases, it felt as if I couldn't catch my breath. My heart began to pound and my pulse began to race. It seemed as if I had just completed a marathon and there was no oxygen left. "Where will I go? Where can I turn? Why doesn't anyone care what they are doing to me? Do I matter so little to these people in whom I had invested my very life?"

The rest of the verse was a comfort, but little did I know that it would be prophetic in my life: "The LORD answered me and set me in a large place." Quite literally the LORD rescued the psalmist out of the place of choking where he couldn't catch his breath. That is what I needed. A large place, a spacious place so that I could rest and catch my breath. Somewhere safe, a place of truth where I did not have to defend myself.

While 118:5 would prove to be prophetic, it was 118:6 that lifted my spirit: "The LORD is for me; I will not fear; What can man do to me?" Oh, glorious verse. Oh, magnificent Word. Oh, Declaration Divine. Yes, the LORD is for me. . . . In all honesty, what can man do to me?

The question became, how do I make this my own? How can I arrive in this place? My eyes went back to the beginning of the psalm, and it gave me a simple path to wisdom. In the very first verse the psalmist gives to us a prayer and a promise: "Give thanks to the LORD, for He is good; For His lovingkindness is everlasting." I could feel the Spirit impressing on my heart that I was to get up every day and give thanks. Regardless of what came about that day, I was to give thanks. How could I thank God for what was going on? Was it possible to be thankful for pain, hurt, attacks, lies, and suffering? While that might be difficult, it was possible to be thankful that God is *for* me and that His lovingkindness is everlasting. *Start with that,* I thought . . . and so I did. I found God's wisdom in crisis.

Puzzle Pieces

When my kids were small, I would buy them large-piece puzzles. Each contained maybe twelve pieces, and I would help them put the puzzle together until they could do it on their own. Over the years we graduated to the 2,000- and 3,000-piece puzzles of wheat fields or Christmas wrappings or Mayberry, USA. We would get together and we all would contribute, but at some point, the youngest child would get frustrated. Then it would spread to the older ones. They would eventually say, "I don't know where these pieces go." Somewhere in their frustration they would just start saying, "I am going to put this piece right here." They would then try to force the pieces to go together. I would stop them before they tore the piece by trying, in their frustration, to make it fit. I would have to explain to them that to force a puzzle piece to go where it is not made to go will throw the entire picture out of whack. Soon none of the pieces would fit together. Too often in crisis, we do just that. We attempt to make the pieces go where we want them to go. In the end, we have a totally distorted situation. It looks nothing like what it was created to be.

In my crisis, I had to slow down and decide that God was big enough to handle the situation and to handle me. He was also big enough to handle the others without me trying to enact my own justice on them. I came to what I can only describe as an elegant peace because of the wisdom of God. God led me from what was a stranglehold on my life into the broadest plain that I have ever walked.

In the chapters ahead, I will take you through a series of biblical events that happened to real people, in real situations. You will see yourself in them. You also will find pearls of Godly wisdom scattered all about. Don't keep your eye so much on the people in the passages. Keep your eye on God.

1

Growing in Wisdom

Why do smart people do dumb things? Several years ago, Mortimer Feinberg and John Tarrant wrote a book addressing this question. Based on their research, they noted, "Risks increase with IQ and status. The smarter you are, and the more you've accomplished, the greater the risk."[1] While the authors go on to lay out a multitude of reasons why smart people do dumb things, the primary reason seems to be that people rely too much on their own smarts.

Solomon, the wisest man who ever lived, taught this:

> Trust in the Lord with all your heart, And do not lean on your own understanding.
> In all your ways acknowledge Him, And He will make your paths straight. (Prov. 3:5-6)

We long for wisdom; we read books on wisdom; we go to seminars on how to make wise decisions, and yet we struggle in our daily lives because it feels like we are making important, critical decisions by the seat of our pants. Where do we find wisdom?

---

1. Mortimer R. Feinberg and John J. Tarrant, *Why Smart People Do Dumb Things* (New York: Simon & Schuster, 1995), 12.

How can it be acquired? What is wisdom, understanding, and knowledge? Are they alike or are they different? Through this book, we will discuss these questions and find biblical answers enabling us to make wise decisions in our everyday lives.

The Word of God speaks a great deal about godly wisdom and gives us examples of it in the lives of many characters in scripture. The Bible also shows us examples of worldly wisdom and the disastrous outcomes that ensue when we lean on our own understanding. James speaks of a worldly wisdom that is not from above but is "earthly, sensual, devilish" (James 3:15, KJV). It was this worldly wisdom that Satan offered in the garden through the fruit of the tree of knowledge of good and evil:

> When the woman saw that the tree was good for food, and that it was a delight to the eyes, and that the tree was desirable to make one wise, she took from its fruit and ate; and she gave also to her husband with her, and he ate. (Gen. 3:6)

The decision to follow worldly wisdom was calamitous and catastrophic, and it brought about the fall of humankind and this universe. The wisdom this world offers leads ultimately to death. Paul tells us that the wisdom of this world is foolishness to God (1 Cor. 3:19).

God's wisdom can be seen in the Tree of Life. In fact, Proverbs 3:18 says wisdom "is a tree of life to those who take hold of her." Proverbs also tells us that wisdom is born out of the fear of the LORD (Prov. 1:7). The wisdom of God created this world: "The LORD by wisdom founded the earth, By understanding He established the heavens" (Prov. 3:19).

What is wisdom? The word for wisdom in Greek is *sophia* In Hebrew, it is the word *hokma*. These words speak of godly wisdom—the wisdom that created everything and comes from God Himself through His Word. Wisdom is wedding your knowledge to the Word of God to make competent, godly, discerning decisions in life.

When we think of acquiring wisdom and those who had godly wisdom, our minds usually go to Solomon. But Luke 2 tells us that Jesus grew in wisdom. In Luke 2:40 we read: "The Child continued to grow and become strong, increasing in wisdom; and the grace of God was upon Him."

That Jesus "grew in wisdom" speaks to the human nature of Christ. Jesus was fully God and fully man at the same time, part of the mystery of the incarnation. As fully divine, He was omniscient, but omniscience does not grow in wisdom. As a boy, and then a young man, Jesus was growing in wisdom. We know that Jesus based every move He made on the Word of God, so it is ludicrous for us to presume that we could be wise without also being immersed in the Word.

We see that Jesus was immersed in the Word in the very next event mentioned in Luke 2, in which Jesus goes with His parents up to Jerusalem for the Feast of the Passover. This is one of the most familiar New Testament stories, but let's look at its context. Luke first tells us that Jesus was increasing in wisdom, and then he shows it, as we see the boy Jesus sitting in the midst of the teachers. We find this story in Luke 2:

> Now His parents went to Jerusalem every year at the Feast of the Passover. And when He became twelve, they went up there according to the custom of the Feast; and as they were returning, after spending the full number of days, the boy Jesus stayed behind in Jerusalem. But His parents were unaware of it, but supposed Him to be in the caravan, and went a day's journey; and

they began looking for Him among their relatives and acquaintances. When they did not find Him, they returned to Jerusalem looking for Him. Then, after three days they found Him in the temple, sitting in the midst of the teachers, both listening to them and asking them questions. And all who heard Him were amazed at His understanding and His answers. When they saw Him, they were astonished and His mother said to Him, "Son, why have You treated us this way? Behold, Your father and I have been anxiously looking for You." And He said to them, "Why is it that you were looking for Me? Did you not know that I had to be in My Father's house?" (Luke 2:41-49)

Jesus is our example in all things, including godly wisdom. In Jesus, "all the treasures of wisdom and knowledge" are hidden (Col. 2:3). At just twelve years old, Jesus shows us one of the first principles of wisdom—to fulfill the will of the Father.

Godly wisdom starts with our desire to fulfill the will of the Father. Godly wisdom is not God showing us the future or revealing His itinerary to us ahead of time. Godly wisdom is not God giving us answers to hard questions to trivia so we can dazzle our fellow office workers. Godly wisdom is not God imparting to us winnable arguments to best our brother-in-law in the next family discussion. Godly wisdom humbles us and causes us to trust God for every decision in life, even when it means keeping our mouths shut and saying nothing. David said he would "guard his mouth with a muzzle" in Psalm 39:1. That is wisdom. How did Jesus grow in wisdom? We find two keys in Luke 2.

Jesus put Himself in the place and position of learning. The bar mitzvah was not initiated as a coming-of-age ritual for Hebrew boys until sometime after Christ's earthly ministry. During the first century, however, Hebrew young men were considered "sons of the law" at the age of thirteen. The rabbis encouraged fathers to bring their sons up to the temple at Passover to prepare them a few years ahead of time for what they would encounter. This is most likely why Jesus was with his parents at the Feast of Passover at twelve years old.

At some point, Jesus walked into a discussion of the διδασκαλοσ—the rabbis who taught the Old Testament law. He sat down in the midst of these teachers, which is the place of learning, and there assumed the position of learning.

One of the great issues of our day is that few seem to want to put themselves in the place of learning or in a position to be taught. In December 2022, students at New York City's elite New School insisted every student be given a final grade of A in every subject: "We demand that every student receives a final course grade of A as well as the removal of I/Z grades for the Fall 2022 semester," the first demand reads. "Attendance shall have no bearing on course grade."[2] How many of us would want one of these students to treat us medically or to advise us financially?

We need to be in a place and position of learning because wisdom does not come all at once. Luke 2:40 says that Jesus grew, αυζανω, in wisdom. The Greek word for *grew* is in the imperfect active, which means it was a process. Jesus was filled with wisdom in a way that was ongoing. God does not open our head and pour wisdom in all at once. Wisdom comes through a process. It came that way for Solomon, and it came that way for Jesus.

We see evidence of this later in Luke 2:52 as well, which says Jesus "grew in wisdom." The Greek word used in this passage, however, is different than one used earlier. While Luke 2:40 says

---

2. College Fix Staff, "Elite private college students demand all A's for their fall classes," *College Fix*, December 18, 2022., https://www.thecollegefix.com/elite-private-college-students-demand-all-as-for-their-fall-classes/.

Jesus was "filled," Luke 2:52 says that Jesus "grew." The verb is in the imperfect active indicative and describes a continuous action that happened in the past.

Jesus was no doubt taught the Word of God in His home. God used the continuous action of teaching the Word of God in Jesus' home to help Him grow in wisdom. That's a word for parents today. We will look at that in more detail in the next chapter as we seek to help our children grow in wisdom.

Jesus was growing in wisdom and put himself in the place and position of learning. When Jesus sat down in the midst of the rabbis, He joined them not to match but to listen and engage as they discussed the Torah. Jesus, the sum of all universal wisdom, went to the place of wisdom, the Temple, and put Himself in the position of a student. He listened as they spoke and debated the Word of God. They did not debate whether it was the Word of God, as the rabbis believed that without question. They debated its interpretation. Jesus would have listened and engaged as they discussed what God meant in particular passages and how to apply it to this life.

The Bible is the supreme source of God's wisdom. His wisdom comes to us through His Word. God breathed it into human language and human minds (2 Tim. 3:16-17). Just as my voice is carried through my breath over vocal cords, so God spoke, and man wrote under inspiration.

Jesus listened to these teachers as they discussed the breathed-out Word God had sent to them. He engaged His mind. It is the height of laziness to think we can obtain godly wisdom without a commitment to His Word, to study it and put ourselves in the place and position where our minds will engage with it. While Eastern mysticism teaches adherents to completely empty their minds and clear all thoughts, God expects us to engage our minds, not suspend them. Scripture says we are to be "filled with the knowledge of His will in all spiritual wisdom and understanding, so that you will walk in a manner worthy of the Lord, to please Him in all respects, bearing fruit in every good work and increasing in the knowledge of God (Col. 1:9-10).

You see, we are to put ourselves in the place where we can hear God's Word from the position of a student where we can engage our minds with it. Luke goes on to show us a second key principle for growing in wisdom.

Jesus presented himself to the purposes of God for his life. Wisdom shows up in how we live our lives, the decisions we make, and the choices we select. Jesus knew this, and His actions reflect that He knew the purpose for his life. In John 5:19, Jesus said, "Truly, truly, I say to you, the Son can do nothing of Himself, unless it is something He sees the Father doing; for whatever the Father does, these things the Son also does in like manner."

Doing what reflects the purpose of God for our lives is wisdom.

When Joseph and Mary found Jesus sitting with the teachers, they were astonished and asked, "Why have you treated us like this? . . . Your father and I have been anxiously looking for you" (Luke 2:48). Jesus responded with the first recorded words of the Lord we have: "Why is it that you were looking for Me? Did you not know that I had to be in My Father's house?" (Luke 2:49).

Jesus answered his mother's question with a question. It's almost as if He was surprised that they wouldn't know where He would be. Didn't they know, he asked them, that He was to be about "My Father's business?" The word for "know" means to perceive, to be aware of, to know that this was what He was called to do. Did Jesus understand at this time who He was? I believe so. When He said, "I had to be about My Father's business," He understood his father was not Joseph but God. He was also communicating that He knew He was on earth for a task that was His Father's business—God's plan and purposes.

Godly wisdom allows us to understand our purpose and call in life. Jesus knew His purpose and the meaning of His life. We see that all throughout the ministry of Christ. We see it when at just twelve years old He sat with teachers of the law, when He was later baptized, when He was tempted in the wilderness, and when He obediently went to the cross. Jesus moves across the pages of the Gospels with a great sense of purpose, meaning, and direction.

When Jesus was driven into the wilderness, He never resisted the leading of the Spirit but followed the direction of the Spirit. That is wisdom.

As He faced down Satan in each of the temptations, He responded with the Word of God. He never interjected His own thoughts or feelings but instead quoted the Word of God, even as Satan misquoted and twisted the Word of God. That is wisdom.

When He walked out to the wilderness, Jesus immediately went to John to be baptized. John, too, was a man of wisdom who understood Jesus' purpose. John pointed Jesus out to the crowd, saying, "Behold the Lamb of God who takes away the sin of the world." And when Christ asked John to baptize Him, John replied, "I need to be baptized by you." But Jesus, knowing His earthly purpose, answered, "Permit it at this time; for in this way it is fitting for us to fulfill all righteousness" (Matt. 3:15).

Jesus knew why He was there, what He was supposed to do, and what the first step in His ministry was to be. In doing this, it fulfilled scripture and the purposes of God. He was also showing He would die and rise again. That is wisdom.

When it came time for Him to go to Jerusalem to be crucified, scripture says He was "*determined* to go to Jerusalem" (Luke 9:51, emphasis mine). I love the way the King James Version states it: "And it came to pass, when the time was come that He should be received up, He steadfastly set His face to go to Jerusalem." Without wondering or pondering or guessing, Jesus knew exactly what He was to do. *That is wisdom.*

Listen, that same wisdom is available to every child of God. It doesn't matter how educated we are, how experienced we are, or how smart we are. Psalm 19:7 says, "The law of the LORD is perfect, restoring the soul; the testimony of the LORD is sure, making wise the simple."

God's wisdom is accessible. James tells us if we ask the LORD for His wisdom, He gives it to us and does not upbraid, fuss, or get angry that we asked (James 1:5). The only way we can make it through this wacky, broken, sinful world is by the wisdom that comes only from God.

In 1803, shortly after the United States made the Louisiana Purchase, President Thomas Jefferson commissioned Meriwether Lewis and William Clark, both soldiers and explorers, to find a passage to the West for the purposes of commerce. How would they find a way from St. Louis all the way to the Pacific Ocean? How would they draw a map with any accuracy, and how would they know which direction to go? Here's the method they relied on to navigate:

> In order to map the progress of the Corps of Discovery, Captains Lewis and Clark needed to know their latitude and longitude, and as the journals tell us, they calculated their position frequently. But

to do so, they had to measure a current position relative to something outside of Earth—the sun or stars.

To determine latitude, the distance north of the equator, all they had to do was measure the height of the sun above the horizon at noon. Since Lewis came prepared with the latest technical instruments (the octant and sextant), this measurement should have been easy. But in real life, it wasn't so simple since the biggest obstacle was actually seeing the horizon. That's not a problem on the open seas. But on land, trees and hills often obscure it.

To solve this problem, Lewis also brought a device called an artificial horizon—typically just a tray of water with a sheet of reflective mica on the surface. Measuring the angle between the sun and its reflection in the mica provided exactly twice the angle between the sun and the horizon.[3]

How were they able to navigate through the unknown? They had to use sources outside of this world. The truth is, so do we. If we are to navigate through this life, through this world, through this crazy maze of culture, we need godly wisdom that is beyond this world but available to each of us.

Reflection Questions

1. What is your current understanding of wisdom? Is wisdom attainable, and if so, how do we get it?

2. How did Jesus grow in wisdom, and how is that an example for us?

3. Have you put yourself in the position and place of learning? How can we do this in our life?

3. National Park Service, "Artificial Horizon: Navigation for the Lewis and Clark Expedition," Lewis and Clark National Historic Trail, last updated August 20, 2018, https://www.nps.gov/articles/artificial-horizon-navigation-for-the-lewis-and-clark-expedition.htm.

4. What is the connection between godly wisdom and studying the Word of God? How can we practically put ourselves in a position to engage our minds with the Word?

5. How is wisdom reflected in following God's purpose for our lives?

Prayer

Father, I want Your wisdom, not to be wise in my own eyes but to glorify You in the relationships and tasks You've given me. Oh, how I need it in this world that pushes its agenda and values. Open my eyes to Your wisdom in my decisions and actions. Thank You for Your Word. Make it my delight to study, to hide in my heart, to believe, and to act on. Thank You that no matter what I face, You have the wisdom I need. I trust in Your ways and Your truth. In Jesus' name, amen.

2

Wisdom in Crisis

Not every choice we make brings a crisis, but every crisis brings about choices. We see this when we come to the opening chapter of Exodus. Pharaoh thought he faced a crisis with the growing number of Hebrews, so he made choices that led to slavery and infanticide. The two Hebrew midwives faced a crisis when Pharaoh commanded that they kill all Hebrew infant boys at birth, and they had to choose whether to obey Pharaoh or God. Jochebed faced a crisis when she delivered Moses and had to make a choice about his life. Every crisis forces us to make choices, and we need wisdom for every one of those choices.

A little more than one hundred years after the Protestant Reformation and death of Martin Luther, few were prioritizing missionary work. Around this time, a young man named Baron Justinian von Welz was born into a wealthy Austrian family.[4] He was educated at the best schools but led a decadent and rebellious lifestyle until he was forty years old. At that point, he faced a personal crisis and made a choice that would change his life

---

4. "Baron Justinian von Welz," GFA Missions, May 9, 2007, https://gfamissions.org/baron-justinian-von-welz/.

forever. He committed his life to Christ and thereafter developed and wrote mission strategy still being used today.

Moses also faced a personal crisis at forty years old that forced him to make choices. Now, scripture tells us very little about Moses' boyhood or young manhood. Exodus skips from his infancy to adulthood at forty years old (Exod. 2:10-2:11). We are told nothing of the years in between because the emphasis is not on Moses but on God.

We do, however, learn several things about Moses' upbringing in Acts (Acts 7:22). First, Moses was educated in all the wisdom of the Egyptians. He trained to become a statesman, military leader, politician, and most likely the next pharaoh. Second, Acts tells us Moses was mighty in word, which means he could express himself well. That's an interesting insight because Moses would later tell God he couldn't speak. Finally, we learn Moses was mighty in deed, which points to his military capability. Josephus records that Moses was so handsome people on the street stopped and stared at him, and laborers would walk away from their work to catch a glimpse of him.

Scripture tells us nothing more about his early years until at forty years old, Moses faced a moment of crisis. The situation is recorded in Exodus 2:11-15:

> Now it came about in those days, when Moses had
> grown up, that he went out to his brethren and looked
> on their hard labors; and he saw an Egyptian beating
> a Hebrew, one of his brethren. So he looked this way
> and that, and when he saw there was no one around, he
> struck and killed the Egyptian, and hid him in the sand.
> Now he went out the next day, and behold, two He-
> brews were fighting with each other; and he said to the
> offender, "Why are you striking your companion?" But

he said, "Who made you a ruler and a judge over us? Do you intend to kill me as you killed the Egyptian?" Then Moses was afraid and said, "Surely the matter has become known!"

Through this crisis, Moses would discover this key: a godly choice expressed through a godly character will result in a godly victory.

We all face moments of crisis throughout our life. In those moments, what helps us make godly choices? What hinders us from making godly choices? We see two guiding elements in the crisis Moses faced in Exodus 2.

Never underestimate the foundation of godly instruction.

Moses was pulled from the water by Pharaoh's daughter, but his mother Jochebed raised him until he was about five years old. She laid a foundation in that little boy he would never forget. He never forgot who he was and who God was, even after years in Pharaoh's palace and years as a prince of Egypt. Acts says this: "But when he was approaching the age of forty, it entered his mind to visit his brethren" (Acts 7:23).

The Greek literally says, "it came up into his heart." This is a lesson for all of us parents. We should never underestimate biblical instruction in the life of our child. We may not see its results until they are forty years old, but we ought never undervalue the Word of God taught to a little child.

As we work at passing godly wisdom to our children, three periods in their lives are critical according to Kurt and Olivia Burner. These periods impact how we teach and guide our children at each of three stages:

1. Imprint Period

This is a season when our children are all ears. They are young and they love knowing what Mom and Dad think. Like little ducklings lined up behind their parents, they accept what their parents say. This period passes quickly so it's imperative we use this time to imprint spiritual truths on their hearts and minds.

2. Impression Period

This is the period from about eight to fourteen years old when the imprinting is gone but the child is still highly impressionable. They are open to direction and influence but no longer accept what we say simply because we say it. They are more influenced by how we live than what we say.

During this period, our children want us to do two things: define what we believe and defend what we believe. They begin to debate, which is not the same thing as arguing. We can use their bent to debate during this period to teach them (1) how to reason through ideas and (2) that engaging only for the sake of argument loses the battle at the outset. Our job as parents is to help them think critically, not emotionally.

3. Coaching Period

By fifteen years old, the window for influence is rapidly closing. This is why godly instruction has to start long before they reach this age. In this period, parents move from teacher to coach, a position we hold the rest of our life.[5]

Coaches get players ready for the game; they don't play the game for them. Good coaches also realize that players learn from their mistakes, not by getting everything right the first time.

---

5. Kurt and Olivia Bruner, *The Family Compass* (Colorado Springs: Chariot Victor Publishing).

Coaches know to let their players struggle because struggling through a problem helps the child learn and develop in ways they never would otherwise.

As a parent and coach, we motivate, encourage, challenge, and advise, but we don't force-feed anything. We review the foundational truths with them again and again. We provide a safe environment for them to learn and grow, with prudent guardrails. Nothing provides a safer environment for a child or teen than rules. They may say they hate them, but reasonable rules provide constancy and boundaries that create the security they need to flourish.

One of the great pictures of this is that Deion Sanders, coach for the Colorado Buffaloes, can be seen coaching and hugging Shedeur Sanders on the sidelines. Shedeur is the CU quarterback, and his dad is the coach. Coaching is very much a part of parenting when a child is older.

The godly instruction Moses received for the first five crucial years of his life made an enduring difference when he later faced decisions in crisis. Hebrews 11 gives us more insight into this decision:

> By faith Moses, when he had grown up, refused to be called the son of Pharaoh's daughter, choosing rather to endure ill-treatment with the people of God than to enjoy the passing pleasures of sin, considering the reproach of Christ greater riches than the treasures of Egypt; for he was looking to the reward. (Heb. 11:24-26)

Moses relinquished all the privileges and benefits he had as the son of Pharaoh's daughter and chose to identify with his people, the Hebrews.

We see this same impact of godly instruction in the life of Daniel. Daniel had been taken into Babylonian captivity. When he was brought into the Babylonian king's training for service, Daniel purposed in his heart not to defile himself (Dan. 1:8). That strength of character came from the imprinting, impressing, and coaching his parents had done with him.

Moses' crisis happened when he came upon an Egyptian beating a Hebrew slave. Exodus 2:11 says, "He went out to his brethren and looked on their hard labors; and he saw an Egyptian beating a Hebrew, one of his brethren." The Hebrew word translated "looked" means more than to see. It means to stare or focus and includes the idea of deep emotion. It implies looking at an action or event and getting caught up and emotionally moved.

These verses give us such insight into why Moses made the choices that he did. This amazing passage says Moses saw the Χριστοσ, which means the anointed, a Savior, a deliverer. No doubt Moses' mother told him God was going to send someone to deliver them. Joseph told his brothers this very thing back in Genesis 50:24-26. Jochebed must have included this as she told the story of Joseph to Moses: ". . . God will surely take care of you and bring you up from this land (Egypt) to the land which He promised on oath to Abraham, to Isaac, and to Jacob." When he identified with his own people, the Hebrews, he very well may have seen himself as the fulfillment of that prophecy. Maybe he thought God had positioned him specifically for this. Take heart, parents—it might take forty years, but at some point, your children will realize God has a purpose and plan for their lives.

Don't overestimate the accomplishments of human achievement.

In all likelihood, Moses recognized what the Egyptian government wanted to do with the Hebrews. He also knew his own story—how his mother had risked everything to save him, and how he'd been kept alive and placed in Pharaoh's palace by God's hand. But then he went a step further. It appears Moses got the idea that the LORD put him in his position to save and deliver the Hebrews. We see that in Acts 7:25: "And he supposed that his brethren understood that God was granting them deliverance through him, but they did not understand."

After Moses killed the Egyptian and buried him to cover up what he'd done, he went back to the scene of the incident the next day. He found two Hebrews fighting and stepped in to break up the fight. One turned and pushed Moses, saying, "Who made you a ruler and judge over us? You do not mean to kill me as you killed the Egyptian yesterday, do you?" (Acts 7:27-28).

Moses had overestimated his accomplishments. He had inflated his abilities. Moses stepped in to break up the fight because he thought he could handle the situation. How often do we step into something feeling sure we have the ability to handle it? We suppose we can accomplish more in our flesh than we can. If we get ahead trying to carry out God's purposes in our own flesh, we will miss God working in us and through us.

God had a purpose and plan for Moses, but Moses trusted his own ability and got ahead of God. We can do that as well. We see seven ways we can hinder God working in us and through us.

1. Moses acted from passion rather than godly principle.

How many times have we allowed our hearts to outrun our heads? Moses was acting out of pure emotion rather than leaning on godly wisdom. When our emotions are triggered, we need to let God's principles lead us instead.

2. Moses moved in his time and not God's time.

Timing is everything. God is working in ways and in places we cannot see. But nowhere in Exodus 2 do we see Moses seeking God's timing. What a difference waiting on God's timing makes.

3. Moses tried to force open a door God had not opened.

When we fail to wait for God's timing, we can force open a door God never intended for us. Striving in our own flesh will cause us to open doors God meant to stay closed and walk past doors God has clearly opened.

4. Moses operated in his way and not in God's will.

God's intended way of deliverance for the Hebrews far exceeded anything Moses could imagine. God would not deliver the Hebrews through Moses' personal accomplishment.

5. Moses took counsel with himself and not with God.

Moses looked around before he killed the Egyptian, but he should have looked up. When we're in a crisis and desperate for wisdom, are we relying on ourselves, on those around us, or are we going to the source of all wisdom?

6. Moses operated out of a personal agenda rather than a godly directive.

It looks as though this was more about Moses than anything else. We can cloak our actions with lofty rationales, but what is our real motive? Our choices should reflect only a godly directive, not our personal agenda.

7. Moses acted in human strength, not godly wisdom.

God's Word says, "not by might nor by power, but by My Spirit, says the LORD of Hosts" (Zech. 4:6). Moses had not yet learned that God's work and purposes are done through God's strength and not our own.

Like Moses, we often overestimate what we can achieve by our own accomplishments. We put our confidence in ourselves, our strength, and our ability. We become enamored with our past achievements, education, and experience. In short, we impress ourselves and inflate what we think we can accomplish. That will always lead to a crisis.

God is going to have to take Moses to the backside of the desert for forty years to get the Moses out of Moses.

God will have to teach Moses that when we make godly choices, regardless of the crisis, we don't have to look around to see who is watching, nor do we have to bury our mistakes.

After Baron von Welz laid out a revolutionary strategy for missions and funded it himself, he reached a crisis. He could find no one to go. That crisis brought about a choice. He'd go himself. Relinquishing his title and inheritance, he said, "What is it to me the title wellborn, when I am born again to Christ? What is it to me the title Lord, when I desire to be the servant of Christ? What is it to me to be called Your Grace, when I have need of God's grace? All these vanities I will away with, and all else I will lay at the feet of my dear LORD Jesus."

Baron von Welz went to Suriname, South America, in 1666, but by 1668 he was dead. No one knows how he died, whether by malaria or native people, or some wild animal. From all accounts, he never led a single person to Christ and never planted a church. He died in obscurity. Yet the mission strategy von Welz developed that motivated his choice in crisis to go is still being used today.

Reflection Questions

1. If you are a parent, are you in the imprint, impression, or coaching period? How does that affect your parenting?

2. We looked at seven ways we can hinder God working in us and through us. Apply each of the following questions to where God has you right now.

Are you acting out of emotion rather than godly wisdom?

Are you moving in your timing rather than waiting on God's timing?

Are you trying to force open a door God has not opened?

Are you operating in your way instead of in God's will?

Are you looking around instead of looking up?

Are you operating out of a personal agenda or God's directive?

Are you acting in human strength or godly power?

Prayer

Heavenly Father, I don't want to make choices from a place of panic but from a place of wisdom. Help me do that as I parent. Help me guard my time and priorities so that I lay a solid foundation for my children in You. Keep me from forcing doors You want closed, and do not let me miss doors You have for me. Give me patience to wait on Your timing, to move in Your will, and to act in Your strength. Give me wisdom not to go ahead of You. In Jesus' name, amen.

3

Wisdom on the Sidelines

From the age of five, Jamie Whitmore knew she wanted to be an athlete and compete in the Olympics. Over the years, she played just about every sport from swimming to fast pitch softball, volleyball, cross-country, and track and field. She became a pro athlete in mountain biking and off-road Xterra triathlons—a sport that includes off-road biking, swimming, and running. By 2004, Jamie was the world champion Xterra triathlete. In fact, over the next seven years, she won thirty-seven championships, more than any other male or female athlete.

In 2008, however, Jamie was diagnosed with a rare form of cancer that wrapped itself around her sciatic nerve. She lost the use of most of her left leg, hamstring, and glute muscle. When the cancer reoccurred, she had surgery and then an emergency room trip because she was so sick. They discovered she was expecting, and the ultrasound showed it was twins.

She'd been sidelined, but this did not stop Jamie. Learning lessons from the sideline, she entered the Paralympics in Rio. She went on to win back-to-back gold medals in the Paralympics. Jamie has remarried and has added two more children from the marriage, making it a home of six. Being a full-time mom of four, she is still competing nationally and internationally, and she is still winning medals.

We can learn a great deal from the sideline if we open ourselves to it. Moses ended up on the sideline. He had blown it big time when he killed the Egyptian who was beating a Hebrew slave and buried him in the sand (Exod. 2:11-12).

Moses thought he was the one to deliver the Hebrews. Perhaps Moses thought helping the slave and killing the abusive Egyptian would endear him to the Hebrews, but it did the opposite. When Pharaoh discovered what happened, he began hunting down Moses like he was the fugitive Dr. Richard Kimble.

While Moses chose to identify with his people, the Hebrews, rather than the Egyptians, he went about it in an ungodly way. He acted in his own strength and got ahead of the LORD. He blew it.

Moses fled for his life from Egypt to Midian in the Sinai. Midian was a wilderness in more ways than one. But here, Moses would learn that even in failure, if we follow the LORD, He will work for us, in us, and in spite of us. God may put us on the bench, but let's not mistake that for being put on the shelf. When God puts us on the bench, He still has a plan and purpose for us.

Maybe you feel like you are in the wilderness. Scripture shows us God does some of his finest work on some of His greatest leaders in the wilderness:

- It was in the wilderness that Jacob saw a stairway to heaven (Gen. 28).

- It was in the wilderness that Elijah heard the still, small voice of God (1 Kgs. 19).

- It was in the wilderness that Elijah was fed by the ravens (1 Kgs. 17).

- It was in the wilderness that John the Baptist learned to preach (Matt. 3).

- It was in the wilderness that Jesus rebuked the devil (Matt. 4).

- It was in the wilderness that Paul searched the scriptures for Christ (Gal. 1:17).

God had intentional purposes for each of these in the wilderness. He has intentional purposes for us as well. Exodus 2 shows us three lessons we need when we find ourselves sidelined.

On the sidelines, we learn that disappointments can be divine appointments. Moses fled Egypt for the Sinai into Midian. Midian was one of six sons of Abraham through his second wife, Keturah, whom Abraham married after Sarah died (Gen. 25:1-2). The Midianites were descendants of Abraham who lived east of the Jordan and Dead Sea through Arabia and into the Sinai.

Scripture says Moses came to a well in Midian and sat down (Exod. 2:15). He must have collapsed against that well, filled with disappointment that his life had come to this. Everything that had been his and everything that would have been his as the adopted son of Pharaoh's daughter was gone. Maybe he replayed over and over the scene where he stepped in to deliver the Hebrew slave and killed the Egyptian. In that moment, Moses likely thought he was following the LORD, doing the LORD a favor, and answering the LORD's need to deliver the Hebrews. Looking at his circumstances, Moses probably thought he had wrecked everything.

But God had Moses right where He wanted him. Moses was no longer in the palace of the pagan Pharaoh, going to the temple of the sun, being taught by the priests of Ra. God had him on the backside of the desert where the living God would take him to school. Instead of gazing up at the pyramids, Moses was going to look up to the mountain of God. Instead of leading an army, Moses would lead sheep and, one day, a nation. Moses was in a place where he would find that life's disappointments can be divine appointments.

In 1463, the city council of Florence, Italy, decided to erect a monument in the city's piazza, the city's center square. They commissioned a sculptor named Agostino di Duccio, who went to the world-famous quarry at Carrara where beautiful, pure-white marble is quarried. He personally marked off a nineteen-foot piece of marble, but when they cut it, they cut it too thin.

As they were moving it, the piece of marble fell, leaving a fracture down the side. The famous sculptor insisted he could only work with a new piece of marble, but the city refused to purchase more. Consequently, that piece of marble was left in the city square on its side for thirty-eight years. It became an embarrassment for the city known as the seat of the Renaissance.

In 1501, the council decided to give another sculptor a chance to create something with the piece of marble. They chose a young sculptor, only twenty-six years old. He took the piece of flawed marble behind the Duomo, the Cathedral, and for three years he chiseled on it until it was finished. It then took forty-nine men five days to move the statue into the city hall, where they unveiled what is considered to be the greatest piece of sculpture in the world, the *David*. The twenty-six-year-old sculptor was Michelangelo, who took a flawed piece of marble and created a masterpiece.[6]

---

6. Sam Whatley, *Pondering the Journey* (Country Club Hills, IL: True Life Publishers, 2002), 17–18.

God specializes in taking the lives of the flawed and the disappointed and scheduling divine appointments. If we respond to Him, He will work for us, in us, and through us so that when He is finished sculpting away the rough edges of flesh and self, He unveils what we never could have imagined in our lives.

On the sideline we learn to be dependent on God rather than independent from God. In Midian, Moses was cut off from the way of life he'd known. Raised in Pharaoh's palace and coddled as a prince of Egypt, Moses had been insulated from feeling any kind of real need. He was young, strong, wealthy, well-educated, and likely unaware he needed anything or anyone.

It was completely different in the desert. He had nothing in the desert—no servants, no palace, no court, and no knowledge of how to survive in the wilderness. God had him in a place where he would have to learn complete dependence on God.

The sideline is often the place where we are able to learn dependence on God in ways we never could when life is comfortable and full. Our hearts are more teachable when we get sidelined. We see this in the parable Jesus told of the soils.

In the parable, a farmer scattered seed. Some fell on hard soil, where birds came and ate it. Some fell on rocky soil, but without roots it quickly withered. Some seed fell on thorny soil and was choked out. And some fell on good soil, where it took root, flourished, and produced a crop (Matt. 13:3-8).

Ray Steadman believed the four soils are not four different people but one person at four different stages. This is the condition of one's heart at different times in life. Sometimes our hearts are hard, and Satan comes and steals away the Word so that we get nothing out of reading or hearing it. Sometimes our hearts are so rocky that the Word cannot take root. Sometimes our hearts are infested with the weeds of this world, choking out the Word. And sometimes our hearts are tilled and prepared, ready to receive the Word and apply it in our lives.[7]

That is why the same sermon can bring one person to the point of tears and decision, while another is constantly looking at the time wondering when it will be over. God often has to sideline us in the wilderness to get our hearts to the place where we leave our independence to become dependent on Him.

On the sideline we learn that God separates us from some things to prepare us for some other things. God is never in a hurry to prepare His servants. Moses' sidelining would take forty years. When Moses collapsed by the well in Midian, he had been prince of Egypt, the largest, most powerful, most developed empire in the world at that time. He was at the very top of the food chain. If this were a Disney movie, he would be Prince Charming. But Moses had two great lessons to learn before God could send him as deliverer.

Humility

In the desert, God placed Moses with the very people the Egyptians despised—shepherds (Gen. 46:34b). Moses was used to leading armies and directing attendants, but God had him leading sheep.

So often when we are sidelined, we never understand why. It is usually because God is trying to separate us from our pride and separate us to humility. Look at these passages:

7. Ray Steadman, *The Gospel of Mark*, vol. 1, ed. James Denney (Grand Rapids: Discovery House Publishers, 2002), 133-134.

- Psalm 10:17: "O Lord, You have heard the desire of the humble; You will strengthen their heart, You will incline Your ear."

- Isaiah 57:15: "For thus says the high and exalted One Who lives forever, whose name is Holy, 'I dwell on a high and holy place, And also with the contrite and lowly of spirit In order to revive the spirit of the lowly And to revive the heart of the contrite.'"

- 1 Peter 5:6: "Therefore humble yourselves under the mighty hand of God, that He may exalt you at the proper time."

God stationed Moses to lead sheep that are prone to wander, not very bright, and easy targets. All three characteristics point to the pride of life. Pride makes us wander, sets us up as an easy target, and proves how dumb we are. Moses would be steeped in lessons of pride and humility for forty years.

Servanthood

Raised as a prince, Moses needed to learn what it meant to be a servant. As soon as Moses sat down at the well, he witnessed another case of injustice. This time it was not an Egyptian beating a Hebrew, but men abusing women. The seven daughters of the priest of Midian had come to water their flocks and gone through the laborious work of filling the troughs. As soon as they were filled, however, the shepherds drove the women away.

Moses intervened on their behalf, but this time he did not kill anyone. Having driven away the men, Moses drew more water for the women's flocks. Now, this was a culture with very strict gender delineations, and drawing water was considered the work of a woman. Moses's actions stand out as a mark of servanthood.

This prince who had been served hand and foot was learning to be a servant.

This points directly to the servanthood of Jesus. Philippians says Jesus did not think His equality with God a thing to be grasped, but emptied Himself and took on the form of a servant (Phil. 2:6-7).

God took forty-year-old Moses at the prime of his manhood, sidelined him, and taught him humility and servanthood for the next forty years.

We look at this and shake our heads at such waste. Why would God sideline someone so strong, so educated, and so gifted in the prime of his life? This is what we need to understand: time spent with God is never time wasted.

Maybe you are sidelined right now. Maybe you feel like this is the prime of your life and it's passing you by because God has sidelined you. Be with Him. Listen to Him. Let Him instruct you. Because time with God on the sideline is preparation for what He wants to do with you, in you, and through you.

John Wesley was also sidelined from time to time and wrote:

> I am no longer my own, but Yours. Put me to what You will, rank me with whom You will; put me to doing, put me to suffering; let me be employed for You or laid aside for You, exalted for You or brought low for You; let me be full, let me be empty; let me have all things, let me have nothing; I freely and wholeheartedly yield all things to Your pleasure and disposal.[8]

Reflection Questions

1. Have you had circumstances in your life that made you feel sidelined? Describe what that was like.

---

8. *The Methodist Service Book* (London: Methodist Publishing House, 1975), D10.

2. How has God used disappointments in your life as His divine appointments? What would you say to someone who is, right now, sitting in deep disappointment?

3. How does the sideline, or the wilderness, teach us to be fully dependent on God? Why is that important?

4. We saw that the sideline separates us from something and for something. What has God separated you from and separated you for as you've been on the sideline?

5. "God is never in a hurry to prepare His servants." How can we embrace the time God has us on the sideline when we don't know how long it will last?

Prayer

Dear LORD, I confess that disappointment is hard and hurtful. The wilderness is not what I would have chosen, but I trust that You have allowed it, and You have much for me in it. Till the hard soil of my heart so that Your Word takes deep root in me, flourishes, and produces much good fruit. Reveal the weeds I've allowed to choke out Your voice and Your wisdom, and help me to root them out completely. I am Yours. You waste nothing. I surrender my plans, my timeline, and my expectations to You. Have Your way with me in this and in all things. In Jesus' name, amen.

4

Wisdom in Waiting

Houston had a problem. A Houston airport had constant passenger complaints about long waits at the baggage claim. Alex Stone, writing for the *New York Times,* explained how airport executives solved the problem. They initially hired more baggage handlers, significantly reducing wait times, but the complaints continued. Looking deeper, they found that passengers took on average one minute to walk from their gate to baggage claim, but then had to wait seven minutes for their luggage. They were waiting seven times longer than they were walking. In a novel solution, the executives moved the arrival gates further from the baggage claim area so that it took longer to get to baggage claim. The passengers walked further but waited less. Passengers were happier, and the complaints virtually stopped.

The time it took baggage to arrive had not changed, but what passengers did while the baggage was arriving did. Stone interviewed MIT professor Robert Larson, a world expert on waiting in lines, who said, "Often the psychology of queuing is more important than the statistics of the wait itself." In other words, it's not how long we wait, but what we do while we wait that matters.

"Occupied time . . . feels shorter than unoccupied time," Stone wrote. When we have something to do while we wait, the wait becomes bearable.[9]

This is part of what makes waiting on God so difficult. It feels like unoccupied time. We begin to question what is happening behind the scenes of our lives. Is God actually doing anything? When we feel as though we have been put on pause, we ask, "What is God doing?"

Waiting on God may feel like unoccupied time, but God is always doing significant work in our wait. In fact, God will reveal Himself to us while we wait on Him. This is part of the wisdom God gives us *as* we wait on Him. We see God reveal Himself in two ways as Moses waited on God.

God gives us the wisdom of knowing Him in our waiting. In Exodus 5:23-6:1-3, we read:

> "Ever since I came to Pharaoh to speak in Your name, he has done harm to this people, and You have not delivered Your people at all." Then the LORD said to Moses, "Now you shall see what I will do to Pharaoh; for under compulsion he will let them go, and under compulsion he will drive them out of his land." God spoke further to Moses and said to him, "I am the LORD; and I appeared to Abraham, Isaac, and Jacob, as God Almighty, but by My name, LORD, . . . I did not make Myself known to them."

This is the second time God came to Moses instructing him to approach Pharaoh and tell him the LORD had said to let His people go. The first time Moses had done this, it resulted in disater. Pharaoh had penalized the Hebrews by adding to their labor. So,

9. Alex Stone, "Why Waiting is Torture," *New York Times*, August 19, 2012, https://www.nytimes.com/2012/08/19/opinion/sunday/why-waiting-in-line-is-torture.html.

the second time God instructed Moses to appear before Pharaoh and tell him God had said to let His people go, Moses prayed and reminded God of what had happened so far: "Ever since I came to Pharaoh to speak in Your name, he has done harm to this people, and You have not delivered Your people at all" (Exod. 5:23).

Moses was essentially saying, "God, your plan did not work, and since then you have done nothing. There's been no deliverance, and we are just sitting and waiting, suffering even more." Moses could not understand why God was not delivering the people as He said He would.

We don't like to wait. Often, by the time we turn to God in prayer, we are desperate for God to move and to move immediately. When God waits in response to our prayers, we become frustrated, agitated, and exasperated with God just as Moses did in Exodus.

Why does God make us wait? He wants to reveal something of His person to us.

We can see this as the passage continues in Exodus 6:2, where God says, "I Am the LORD." He closes this passage with those same words: "I am the LORD" (Exod. 6:8). God brackets what He tells Moses with His self-identification. Four times in eight verses, God declares His name. God's name is a revelation of who He is, past, present, and future.

God's Past Revelation

In Exodus 6:3, God tells Moses that He appeared to Abraham, Isaac, and Jacob as God Almighty, or El Shaddai, the All-Sufficient God. God revealed Himself to the Patriarchs as their sufficiency. God was Abraham's sufficiency when Abraham felt personally inadequate because he was childless. God's sufficiency was reflected when God changed his name from Abram, which meant Exalted Father, to Abraham, meaning Father of a Nation. God was sufficient to bring that about.

God was sufficient for Isaac in his helplessness. After being banished from Gerar, Isaac was out in the wilderness and needed water. The Philistines had filled the wells dug by Abraham, but Isaac dug them out again and hit water. Each time Isaac reopened a well, the sons of Gerar would come and fill it back up. After several such events, Isaac moved into Beersheba, where the LORD appeared to him and said, "Do not fear, for I am with you." There in Beersheba, Isaac's herdsmen dug a well and hit water. God was sufficient for every need of Isaac.

God was sufficient for Jacob as he faced multiple unknowns. After stealing the birthright and with Esau murderously mad, Jacob faced the unknown as he fled to his mother's brother, Laban. When he left Laban after nearly twenty years and went back to Canaan, Isaac faced the unknown when Esau came out to meet him. He faced the unknown of deep loss as his beloved wife, Rachel, died giving birth to Benjamin. He faced an unknown future after news that Joseph had been supposedly killed. And then years later, as an old man, Jacob faced the unknown as he traveled to Egypt in the midst of famine. How would it turn out for Jacob and his sons? Would they be cared for as they went down to Egypt? God proved to be sufficient in every one of these moments of Jacob's life.

In each situation, the patriarchs had to wait on God. They waited for extended periods of time. But they discovered that in the waiting, God revealed Himself to be the All-Sufficient One. This was not unoccupied time. It was invaluable time, in which God revealed wisdom about who He was.

God's Present Identification

God had appeared to Abraham, Isaac, and Jacob as God Almighty, but to Moses and these Hebrews He appeared as LORD, Yahweh (Exod. 6:3). *Yahweh* literally means "I Am." It is the verb of being in Hebrew. This is not a new or different God. God was revealing more of Himself. God was communicating that He was the God who made the covenant with Abraham, and He was still there to enact that covenant with Moses and the Hebrews.

By the end of Joshua's life, after the Hebrews had entered and over time conquered the land, Joshua reflected back over God's covenant faithfulness:

> Now behold, today I am going the way of all the earth, and you know in all your hearts and in all your souls that not one word of all the good words which the LORD your God spoke concerning you has failed; all have been fulfilled for you, not one of them has failed. (Josh. 23:14)

He said the same thing in Joshua 21:45: "Not one of the good promises which the LORD had made to the house of Israel failed; all came to pass."

As Moses waited for God to rescue the Hebrews, God revealed that He was the God who was there, in their present situation and circumstances. He would keep His word, His covenant to Abraham, Isaac, and Jacob, in their day. God declared, "I am the LORD. *I Am.* I am the One who is here right now in the present."

In Exodus 6:5, God said He knew their difficulty and suffering: "Furthermore I have heard the groaning of the sons of Israel, because the Egyptians are holding them in bondage, and I have remembered My covenant." They would experience the fulfillment of God's promises if they learned His wisdom in the waiting, and in that waiting God would reveal something of the wisdom of His person.

You may be waiting on God to do something in your life and your situation. You may be wondering why God doesn't move to help. Just like these great men of God in the past who waited on God to act, God may be revealing something of His person to you as you wait.

God's Plan

God gives us wisdom about His plan in our time of waiting. We learn more about the wisdom that comes in waiting in Exodus 6:6-8:

> Say, therefore, to the sons of Israel, "I am the LORD, and I will bring you out from under the burdens of the Egyptians, and I will deliver you from their bondage. I will also redeem you with an outstretched arm and with great judgments. Then I will take you for My people, and I will be your God; and you shall know that I am the LORD your God, who brought you out from under the burdens of the Egyptians. I will bring you to the land which I swore to give to Abraham, Isaac, and Jacob, and I will give it to you *for* a possession; I am the LORD.

For the second time God said, "I am the LORD" and then set forth the seven "I wills" to the Hebrews. We have already looked at the past and present nature of God's name, Yahweh. Let's now look at the future meaning behind God's revelation. All seven of these "I will" statements are in the future tense. They indicate what Yahweh is going to do.

1. God's Intentionality

God revealed His intentionality in the first three "I will" statements of Exodus 6:6. The LORD first said, "I will bring you out," meaning that He would bring Israel out of the experience of bondage. Secondly, He said, "I will deliver you," meaning He would snatch Israel out of the circumstances of their bondage. Thirdly, God said, "I will also redeem you," conveying that He would purchase them from their situation.

In their waiting, the Hebrews were going to see the wisdom of God in His redemptive plan to bring them out of bondage and deliver them. The culmination of their deliverance wouldn't take place until some later time. They had to wait through all ten plagues, the Passover, their wilderness trek to the Red Sea, and then the Red Sea crossing, but there, God said He would deliver them completely: "for the Egyptians whom you have seen today, you will never see them again forever" (Exod. 14:13).

God's deliverance out of Egypt is a picture of the great deliverance and redemption Jesus Christ would bring because God's wisdom of intentionality is to bring us out, deliver us and redeem us to Himself.

2. God's Intimacy

God revealed His intimacy in the next two "I will" statements. The LORD said, "I will take you for My people" and "I will be your God." These are words a bridegroom would say to his bride. It is covenant language. It is a word of intimacy to say, "I will take you, you will be mine, and I will be yours."

3. God's Inheritance

In the last two "I will" declarations, God revealed their inheritance. God promised "to bring [them] into the land" and to "give it to [them] for a possession." God was telling the Hebrews to wait on Him and learn His wisdom, and in so doing, they would become possessors of the Promised Land. God was again not only giving these Hebrews a specific promise but picturing the inheritance of heaven promised to us through Christ.

That was all God's plan. We, too, want to know, What is God's plan for me? In waiting for God, we discover the wisdom of His plan over ours. The question becomes, will we listen?

The Hebrews would not listen: "So Moses spoke thus to the sons of Israel, but they did not listen to Moses on account of their despondency and cruel bondage" (Exod. 6:9).

The problem was not really the waiting. The problem was that the Hebrews were enslaved to their slavery. They had become enslaved to their circumstances. Their situation dictated to them what they would hear and what they would shut out. All their direction was coming from within, so that they could not hear the voice of God from without. What kept them in bondage was bondage itself.

What keeps us from hearing the wisdom of God? Our sin and disbelief. We can get so oppressed by sin, so caught up in cycles of sin, that there seems to be no other way. Wisdom of this world will cause us to stop up our ears to God's Word and teaching.

But look at God's response to their stubbornness: "Now the LORD spoke to Moses, saying, 'Go, tell Pharaoh king of Egypt to let the sons of Israel go out of his land'" (Exod. 6:10-11). God's plan is not dependent on our response. His plan is not dependent on whether we listen to Him or not. His plan will not be frustrated. It behooves us, however, to listen to the voice of God. That is wisdom.

When God reveals Himself to us in the waiting, we have a choice to listen or not. Erwin McManus tells this story about his son:

My son, Aaron, was five or six when he began asking me, "What does God's voice sound like?" I didn't know how to answer.

A few years later, Aaron went off to his first junior high camp. In the middle of the week, I went up with another pastor at Mosaic to see our kids. Aaron, I learned, had started to assault another kid but had been held back by his friends. He was unrepentant, wanted to leave camp, pulled together his stuff, and shoved it into the car.

I asked him for a last talk with me before we drove away. We sat on two large rocks in the middle of the woods.

"Aaron," I asked, "is there any voice inside you telling you what you should do?"

"Yes," he nodded.

"What's the voice telling you?"

"That I should stay and work it out."

"Can you identify that voice?"

"Yes," he said immediately, "It's God."

It was the moment I'd waited for. "Aaron," I said, "do you realize what just happened? You heard God's voice. He spoke to you from within your soul. Forget everything else that's happened. God spoke to you, and you were able to recognize him."

I will never forget Aaron's dug-in response: "Well, I'm still not doing what God said."

I explained to him that it was his choice, but this is what would happen. If he rejected the voice of God coming from deep within and chose to disobey his guidance, his heart would become hardened, and his ears would become dull.

If he continued on this path, there would be a day when he would never again hear the voice of God. There would come a day when he would deny that God even speaks or has ever spoken to him.

But if he treasures God's voice however it comes to him—through the Scriptures, through his conscience—and responds to him with obedience, then his heart would be softened, and his ears would always be able to hear the whisper of God into his soul.[10]

---

10. Erwin McManus, *The Barbarian Way* (Nashville: Thomas Nelson, 2005), 87-89.

Aaron decided that day to listen to that voice deep within that was not his voice but God's voice, and he stayed.

How about you? Do you hear that still, small voice? If we do not listen to God's Word, we will never know God's wisdom. God's wisdom often comes after God causes us to wait.

Reflection Questions

1. Are you in a season of waiting right now? Describe your wait.

2. Does your wait feel like unoccupied time, or can you see God working as you wait?

3. How has God revealed Himself to you as you wait?

4. In what ways have you seen God as the All-Sufficient One?

5. Have you heard God's still, small voice? What keeps you from listening to God?

6. What has helped you listen and trust His still, small voice?

7. What verse from this chapter is impacting you right now as you wait on God?

Prayer

LORD, thank You for all the times You have been my sufficiency. Thank You for each time You have provided for me, guided me, sustained me, and cared for me. Help me to surrender my whole heart and every plan to You. I give it all to

You and trust You as I wait. Draw me to You and open my eyes to see and know You more fully. Help me listen and obey when You speak. And let this time be used for You, Your glory, and Your purposes. In Jesus' name, amen.

5

Wisdom in Unfairness

Their rivalry is well known and historic in proportion. Antonio Salieri was an Italian classical composer, conductor, teacher, and court musician. He was only twenty-four years old when the Austrian emperor Joseph II appointed him as court musician. His students included noteworthy musicians such as Ludwig van Beethoven, Franz Shubert, and Franz Liszt. Antonio knew his gifts were from God, and along with his many operas, he wrote sacred music as well.

But then along came a very ungodly, ungrateful young man, as Salieri saw him, named Wolfgang Amadeus Mozart. His gifts seemed unparalleled. He was a genius with tremendous gifts and abilities, and yet despite all this, he showed no reverence to God. Salieri could not understand why God had so gifted a sinner while giving Salieri what seemed to be lesser abilities.[11]

Salieri lived a chaste and pious life, but his music was eclipsed by that of a profligate sinner. Salieri became jealous, and that jealousy grew and deepened. Then, tragically, Mozart mysteriously died. Some claimed Salieri had poisoned him, but history and

---

11. *Amadeus*, directed by Miloš Forman (Warner Brothers, Orion Pictures, Warner Home Video, 1984), DVD.

facts do not bear that out. In the movie *Amadeus*, about the rivalry between Salieri and Mozart, the camera pans to Salieri's eyes gleaming after learning of the death of Mozart, as Salieri sits in an insane asylum where he curses God for unfairly denying him the gifts He gave to Mozart.

Life can sometimes seem so unkind and cruel. It's hard enough to deal with the consequences of our own missteps, miscalculations, and mistakes, but it becomes nearly unbearable to deal with hardship that wasn't our fault or that we didn't deserve.

We usually have three responses to the unfairness in our life: First, we blame others. This usually sows the seed of bitterness that often lead to revenge. Second, we feel sorry for ourselves. Life becomes a pity party. We whine to anyone with a sympathetic ear and then begin to wallow in despondency and become immobile, unable to move on because of depression. Third, we stuff our feelings. We just simmer on the inside while telling everyone that nothing is wrong. *We're fine.* But when we stuff our emotions long enough, they emerge as anger and frustration toward people around us who do not deserve it. We become the ones treating others unfairly.

In the fascinating book of Ecclesiastes, Solomon talks about the unfairness of life. Ultimately, Solomon calls us to lean on the wisdom of God rather than surrender to unfair circumstances of life.

Solomon begins by pointing out how unfair life can seem because "it is the same for all" (Eccles. 9:2). This is where the struggle with unfairness begins. Solomon says there is one fate for the righteous and one for the wicked, one for the clean and the unclean, for the one who sacrifices and the one who does not sacrifice, for the good man and for the sinner, for the one who swears and the one who is afraid to swear. You can almost see Solomon shaking his head in perplexity as he claims how evil it is that all men have the same fate—they all die.

We cannot control whether we will face unfair situations in our lives, but we can control our response to those unfair circumstances. Instead of blaming, or stuffing, or feeling sorry for ourselves, wisdom helps us deal with injustice in a godly way.

Wisdom in Unfair Circumstances

Wisdom tells us that unfair circumstances don't have to determine our lives. Solomon claims that one fate awaits all of us—death. He says it is unfair that the good end up in the same place as the bad. But Solomon's claims don't hold up under scripture. The New Testament tells us that there is a difference, not between good and bad, but between saved and unsaved, and that those who have trusted Jesus Christ as LORD and Savior spend eternity in a prepared place called heaven.

Solomon was looking at the kind of unfair situations in life that we all deal with. He argued that once you are dead, you are dead. There could be no more passion, no more love or hate or life: "Surely a live dog is better than a dead lion," he observed, using hyperbole to press his point about the finality and unfairness of life.

But a seemingly unfair situation does not have to determine how we live life. Let's look at three ways godly wisdom helps us deal with inequitable situations of life.

1. Possess the simple pleasures of life.

Ecclesiastes 9:7 says, "Go then, eat your bread in happiness and drink your wine with a cheerful heart; for God has already approved your works." We are to savor certain moments in life. We are to appreciate and cherish these moments, like times around the table with family enjoying a meal or enjoying fellowship with the ones we love. It is a simple thing, a daily activity that becomes a blessing if we allow it to be.

My dad always ensured supper time was special. He would not allow any kind of upset or negative talk, no unkind or offensive conversation whatsoever. It was to be a happy time for the entire family at the end of a day regardless of how the day went. Supper always began with us joining hands in prayer, and for me, it is one of the great memories of my life growing up. The seemingly unfair does not determine our life when we seize the simple pleasures in life.

2. Celebrate the moments of life.

In the next verse, Solomon says, "Let your clothes be white all the time," referring to celebration dress, and "let not oil be lacking on your head," pointing to a fragrant balm that soothed dry skin (Eccles. 9:8). Oil on the skin was necessary to combat the burning wind, the blistering sun, and the arid climate. It spoke of something refreshing. A current-day comparison would be men putting on an after-shave or women applying lotion and perfume and then dressing up in the finest of evening wear. It would be like the Crawleys dressing for dinner every evening at Downton Abbey. Every day was to be a celebration of life.

God does not give us life to live it under a dark cloud. We are not to walk around like we are headed to an execution. We are to embrace life and not allow unfair situations to dictate our attitudes, our responses, or our dispositions. This is how wisdom directs us through daily life in an unfair world.

3. Enjoy your marriage.

Solomon's third counsel is this: "Enjoy life with the wife whom you love" (Eccles. 9:9). Tragically, we are reaping what we have sown in this country—the breakdown of the family. Now a woke generation is redefining the meaning of marriage altogether, further adding to the decline in society.

Solomon used an unusual word here for "enjoy." It's the Hebrew word *rā'â*, which means "to behold, to look at, to consider, to perceive, out of which comes joy." The concept is to focus on your wife, putting your attention and energy there. By investing in your marriage, you will enjoy the dividends.

My mom and dad were married for seventy years and died a little more than six months apart. Their lives were wrapped up with Jesus Christ, each other, and their children. They celebrated life together every day. They literally sought each other's best interest over their own. My dad taught us to respect our mother, and our mother constantly taught us to honor our dad.

My dad had only an eighth-grade education, yet he owned a very successful furniture business. He had a godly wisdom out of which he operated that I envy to this day. He was a man's man, boxed golden gloves, went in at Utah Beach in the invasion of France, and unloaded Patton at Cherbourg. He walked with the LORD. Often, as I would get up in the middle of the night to get a drink of water, I would see him kneeling in the den praying through the night. Life was not about the upsets or unfair treatment this world can give, but a celebration of God and enjoyment of his marriage and family.

Don't let the unfairness of life rob you of what God has given you. Let the celebration of God's goodness outshine the inconsistencies and injustices of life.

Wisdom in Handling the Unpredictable

Wisdom enables us to handle the unpredictable. There's an unpredictable nature to life that so often seems unfair. We expect those who are talented and gifted, those who work hard and do what is right, to do well, but Solomon says it's not always that way:

> I again saw under the sun that the race is not to the swift and the battle is not to the warriors, and neither is bread to the wise nor wealth to the discerning nor favor to men of ability; for time and chance overtake them all. (Eccles. 9:11)

The word *overtake* can mean "to befall, to bring about, to cause, to fall on." It conveys the idea that the unpredictable happens in life. We think the fastest runner should win the race, and the greatest warrior should win the battle. We believe the smartest people become the wealthiest people, but these statements aren't always true.

Solomon says that men can get trapped by unfair circumstances like fish in a net or birds in a snare (Eccles. 9:12). No one sets out to be trapped or ensnared; it usually happens when least expected. We assume our gifts, talent, ability, winsomeness, and smarts will keep us out of any unfair or unjust situation. So, when something does happen, we get angry, frustrated, and bitter as we focus on the injustice and unfairness of life. It all feels very unpredictable.

Mickey Mantle died in August of 1995. He was one of the last of the legendary American baseball players from the days of the greats. Mantle was one of my heroes, yet I never knew about his personal life until just before his death. Mantle said all of his life, all he wanted to do was play baseball and that God had given him the ability to play exceptionally. But he threw it all away, as he became an alcoholic. His wife became an alcoholic as well, and their marriage deteriorated, and tragically their four sons became alcoholics. He stumbled from one affair and drink to the next until he became gravely ill.

In 1995, Mantle underwent a liver transplant but within weeks took a turn for the worse. In desperation, he called his teammate and friend, Bobby Richardson, a well-known Christian who played with Mantle all his career. In fact, the two had played in seven World Series games together. After talking with Richardson, Mickey Mantle gave his life to Jesus Christ, dying only days later.[12]

Mantle had built his life on his abilities, his charm, his all-American good looks, and his hard work. But in the end, that cost him everything. He was unprepared for what his lifestyle brought him. By the time he came to Christ, it was too late to turn around the consequences of living based in worldly wisdom. A key principle of godly wisdom is this: don't wait until it's too late for godly wisdom to be effective in your life.

Just as wisdom will prepare us for the unpredictable, wisdom shows up unpredictably in life. Solomon states in Ecclesiastes 9:13, "Also this I came to see as wisdom under the sun, and it impressed me." Solomon is impressed with wisdom. That's significant because very little ever impressed Solomon. The story of Solomon is well known, however questioned at times. Can a man with this kind of wisdom still sin? The answer unequivocally is yes. His desire for so many wives and concubines makes one question how much wisdom he had. Sin causes a lapse in judgment, to say the least. Most Old Testament theologians believe that Solomon

---

12. Jason Romano, "Mickey Mantle Gave His Life to Christ on His Death Bed," SportsSpectrum.com, August 13, 2017, https://sportsspectrum.com/sport/baseball/2017/08/13/mickey-mantle-gave-life-christ-death-bed/.

wrote Ecclesiastes late in life. He had turned back, evidently, to the LORD who gave him his wisdom. He came back to his senses and expressed great regret for having acted foolishly (see Ecclesiastes 12). Solomon throughout the book of Ecclesiastes is called "Preacher," because he preaches the vanity of following your own wisdom instead of God's. This is why he is considered the wisest man who ever lived—and he is blessed with Godly wisdom.

Solomon tells a story of a small city of few men, besieged by a great king who surrounded the city and constructed large siege works against it (Eccles. 9:14). A poor but wise man lived in it and delivered the city by his wisdom. That is all we are told. The city was saved by wisdom from an unpredictable source, a poor man. What *is* predictable is that the poor man who delivered the city by wisdom was immediately forgotten. But this isn't too surprising. It is an unfair but not unexpected outcome of life.

God, on the other hand, never forgets what we do. It doesn't matter how unseen or small our work is. Jesus noted this when He taught, "And whoever in the name of a disciple gives to one of these little ones even a cup of cold water to drink, truly I say to you, he shall not lose his reward" (Matt. 10:42). While the world may not remember, God never forgets.

Solomon was surprised not only by where wisdom is found but how wisdom triumphs over things that humankind puts confidence in. Solomon wrote that wisdom is better than strength, noise, and fire power (Eccles. 9:16-18). While man thinks he can accomplish great things through strength, thunderous demands, and weaponry, Solomon asserts that wisdom is far more effective than any of these. None of the great king's pseudo-wisdom could stand against wisdom to give him victory over the small city.

Wisdom will prepare us for the unpredictable, even when godly wisdom is unexpected. It is said that George Frederick Handel composed his amazing oratorio *Messiah* in approximately twenty-four days. He wrote the music with failing eyesight while facing the possibility of imprisonment for his outstanding debt. In the midst of these challenges and other difficulties, Handel continued to write until the masterpiece, including the majestic "Hallelujah Chorus," was completed. It was an unexpected and unpredicted brilliance in the midst of the unfairness of life.

Handel later credited the completion of his work to one ingredient: joy. He was quoted as saying that he felt as if his heart would burst with joy at what he was hearing in his mind. Handel, through godly wisdom, was able to navigate the expected and the unpredictable and experienced an explosive internal joy, all because he feared the LORD and leaned on Him.

Every one of us will deal with unfair and unjust situations in life. We cannot avoid them, and we cannot predict them. But godly wisdom allows us to control our response in the situation. The great composer Salieri chose to blame God and spent his last years in misery and bitterness. The great composer Handel chose to let God work in him despite the unfairness. Instead of letting unfairness determine our life, we can trust that God can bring something unforeseeably magnificent through it.

Reflection Questions

1. When you experience unfairness, is your natural tendency to blame, to throw a pity party, or to stuff your emotions? How does trusting God in unfairness help your response?

2. How can you learn to savor the simple moments and celebrate the good moments in life? What impact does it have when we begin to do that?

3. How does wisdom exceed anything man puts confidence in like strength, thunderous demands, or weaponry?

4. In Matthew 10:42, Jesus said, "And whoever in the name of a disciple gives to one of these little ones even a cup of cold water to drink, truly I say to you, he shall not lose his reward." How does the promise of this verse help when we deal with unfairness?

5. Have you seen God bring unforeseen beauty from circumstances that felt unfair at the time, for you or someone else? Describe what God did.

Prayer

Father, we live in a world of unfairness, and yet You have planted us here in the midst of it. We need Your wisdom as we deal with it in our homes, our workplaces, and our neighborhoods. Give us wisdom to know what is right, strength to do what is right, and courage to stand up for what is right. We surrender all outcomes to You. Thank You for Your justice and for Your mercy. Thank You for bringing unforeseen beauty even from unfair circumstances and for seeing what no one else does. We love You, LORD. Help us love You more. In Jesus' name, amen.

6

Wisdom on the Long Road

It was the last number one hit they had. In fact, it was one of the last songs they recorded. Paul McCartney said he sat down at his piano and began tinkering around with some tunes. He was depressed. The breakup of the most successful and famous rock band in history was taking place, and he wrote a sad song.[13] Out of him poured the song, "Long and Winding Road," and he felt like he was living every note of it.

The Beatles could not even agree on how the song was to be recorded. Phil Spector laid down all the tracks, and McCartney hated it.[14] McCartney said about the song "The Long and Winding Road," "It's all about the unattainable; the door you never quite reach. This is the road that you never get to the end of."[15]

---

13. Barry Miles, "2022, February 9," Miles: The Website of Writer Barry Miles, http://barrymiles.co.uk/2022-february-9/.

14. Mike Merritt, "Truth behind ballad that split Beatles," *Sunday Herald*, November 16, 2003, https://web.archive.org/web/20060427062227/http://www.sundayherald.com/38051.

15. Miles, "2022, February 9."

You might say that the Hebrews in Exodus are headed down a long and winding road as well, and an entire generation of them will never reach the end of that road. Exodus 13:17 shows how God led them out of Egypt: "Now when Pharaoh had let the people go, God did not lead them by the way of the land of the Philistines, even though it was near."

God did not take them down the most convenient, stress-free, easy-access road. God intentionally led the Hebrews along a more difficult way. He led them down a long and winding road.

God does the exact same thing with us. And like the Hebrews, we complain and grumble because it's hard, and we do not know what God is doing.

God intends the long and winding road to be a means of blessing and not a means of withholding blessing.

The truth is, very little wisdom ever comes on an easy or comfortable road. While we wouldn't choose the difficult path, godly wisdom comes on the long and winding road.

God's Course

God never consults us about the course on which he leads us. Moses spent forty years in the wilderness. He knew the routes the caravans would take. He knew the roads that no one else could see in the sand. He knew where the water was. However, when the Hebrews came out of Egypt, God did not say to Moses, "Chart us a course, Mr. Sulu."

In Exodus 13, we read that "God did not lead them by the way of the land of the Philistines. . . . God led the people around by way of the wilderness" (Exod. 13:17-18). But this was also true: "The LORD was going before them" (Exod. 13:21). God did not need the Hebrews to chart a course, because He knew exactly where He would and would not lead them. Godly wisdom always has a purpose in how God leads.

The same is true with salvation. No man ever woke up and said, "You know, I am a sinner, and I need a perfect Savior to extend grace to me, die for my sin, and give me His righteousness." That has never happened. The Holy Spirit led that man to a place where he could hear the Word of God and fall under conviction of his sin and lostness. At that point, God didn't ask, "Can you plot a course for your salvation?" No, because God already sent His Son to die for that man's sin. God planned that from the foundation of the world.

In the same way, the LORD never comes and asks us which route in life we would like to take. Look at Jeremiah 29:11, spoken to the nation with a word for us too: "For I know the plans that I have for you," declares the LORD, "plans for welfare and not for calamity to give you a future and a hope."

Our problem is that we keep walking up to God's drafting table with our own set of plans.

How often do we ask, "When is God going to start leading me?" Understand, God never starts leading us until we start following Him. We see this in the story of Abraham's servant going to find a wife for Isaac. When the servant met Rebekah and realized who she was, he thanked God, saying, "I being in the way, the LORD led me" (Gen. 24:27, KJV).

God has already given you plenty of indication about the direction He will lead you. The question is not when He will start leading us, but when will we start following.

God's Direction

God never checks with us about his direction. When God led the Hebrews out of Egypt, He led them down to Succoth. God then turned them farther south and closer to the sea until they eventually camped right against the edge of the Red Sea at Baal-Zephen. We get an indication of the long and winding road God was leading them on in Exodus 14:3: "For Pharaoh will say of the sons of Israel, 'They are wandering aimlessly in the land; the wilderness has shut them in.'"

God was creating an impression for Pharaoh that the Hebrews had no idea what they were doing or where they were going. In other words, they were trapped and sitting ducks.

The Hebrews must also have been wondering what God was doing. This direction made no sense at all. We can find ourselves in that same situation. When we're on a path that doesn't make any sense, do we keep following the LORD? God has told us:

> For My thoughts are not your thoughts, nor are your ways My ways," declares the LORD. For *as* the heavens are higher than the earth, so are My ways higher than your ways and My thoughts than your thoughts. (Isa. 55:8-9)

God's directions don't always make sense to us. For example, God tells us to love our enemies. That doesn't make sense to the Western mind. Love our enemies? Do good to those who mistreat us? That seems absurd. But Jesus taught:

> Blessed are you when *people* insult you and persecute you, and falsely say all kinds of evil against you because of Me. Rejoice and be glad, for your reward in heaven is

great; for in the same way they persecuted the prophets who were before you. (Matt. 5:11-12)

Have people ever attacked you, insulted you, or embarrassed you? I have had it done to me. What does Jesus say? You are blessed, so rejoice and be glad. We have to trust the direction the LORD is leading us even when it goes against our own reasoning.

The path God directs us on may not make sense to us, but it will always bring Him glory. We see that so clearly in Exodus, a book all about God and His glory. Why did God lead the Hebrews on such a long and winding road? So that the Egyptian army would follow after them, and God would be honored—glorified—through it (Exod. 14:4).

The path God directs us to brings Him glory. Our lives are about far more than a paycheck. Our marriages are about far more than staying together. Our churches are about far more than attending. They are to show God's glory. Similarly, God's direction for us is about far more than a destination. As God directs us and we follow, it is about His glory.

God's Call

God always calls us to walk by faith. While God almost never consults us about the course He takes us on, nor asks us for directions, He does call us to follow by faith. He calls us to be obedient and follow Him.

Coming out of Egypt, the Hebrews followed God and eventually found themselves in a trap. But what often looks like a trap to us is God's cradle of care. God had led the Hebrews to the exact spot where He wanted them. At the first hint of trouble, however, their faith fell apart. As soon as they spotted Pharaoh and his army on their heels, they panicked. The rise of fear often causes the loss of faith. Look at the response of the Hebrews:

> As Pharaoh drew near, the sons of Israel looked, and behold, the Egyptians were marching after them, and they became very frightened; so the sons of Israel cried out to the Lord. Then they said to Moses, "Is it because there were no graves in Egypt that you have taken us away to die in the wilderness? Why have you dealt with us in this way, bringing us out of Egypt? Is this not the word that we spoke to you in Egypt, saying, 'Leave us alone that we may serve the Egyptians'? For it would have been better for us to serve the Egyptians than to die in the wilderness." (Exod. 14:10-12)

The proper noun *Egypt* is used over and over like a chorus. Five times we see it in this passage. When our faith is gone, we immediately forget what God has said and what God has done and focus on the flesh.

Satan never gives up without a fight. Satan persists even though he has been defeated over and over again. He will not give up, though at Calvary and the empty tomb he was defeated. He is like a snake that, with a crushed head still moves about giving the impression of life. Have you found that to be true in your life? Even when we have surrendered to Christ and we are following the Lord's direction, the enemy constantly comes back to challenge our commitment. He knows that if he can get us focused on our fears and insecurities, then our faith will falter. Like the Egyptians, we will yearn for the comfort of our old lifestyle.

As their faith wavered, Moses responded by saying, "Do not fear!" (Exod. 14:13). This is what grammarians call a negative imperative, and it is the strongest way to express a negative in Hebrew. Moses was not trying to comfort them; he was rebuking them. He was indicating that they had no reason to fear. He went on to say, "Stand by and see the salvation of the LORD which He will accomplish for you today" (Exod. 14:13b). It was a clear command to get their eyes off the Egyptians and to focus on the LORD. They were to be people of faith.

Not only did Moses charge them to trust in the LORD, but the Hebrews had something in their midst that shouted for them to have faith and trust the LORD. They were carrying the bones of Joseph.

When Joseph was dying, he made the Hebrews swear that they would take his bones up from Egypt and bury them in the land of Canaan. Joseph's request shows us three things as we follow God's leading:

1. Joseph expressed his faith.

In Genesis 50:24, Joseph told his family he was about to die but that God would continue to take care of them. Even on his deathbed, Joseph expressed his faith.

2. Joseph encouraged faith.

Hebrews 11:22 is a fascinating verse that speaks of Joseph: "By faith Joseph, when he was dying, made mention of the exodus of the sons of Israel, and gave orders concerning his bones." Joseph was speaking of the exodus that was to come, encouraging them to have faith that God would deliver them.

3. Joseph extended his faith.

Joseph's faith reached through the generations and influenced those coming after him to trust God by faith. Our influence continues even after we die (Heb. 11:4). Joseph was embalmed in Egypt and placed in a coffin, but scripture doesn't record that he was buried (Gen. 50:26). In a land known for its tombs, no tomb was made for Joseph.

I am certain that his sarcophagus sat out in the open. He was embalmed, most likely mummified, but not interred. I believe his sarcophagus was left out to remind the Hebrews of God's promise that He would come and get them and take them to the Promised Land.

What an incredible legacy to leave. It speaks to us. God will one day come in a generation where believers are threatened by the devil himself, and yet Jesus is going to come and take the dead and living out of this place and carry us over to a new place that He has prepared for us.

If it were up to us, we would all choose the easiest, most comfortable, most direct paths for our life. But very little wisdom comes on the easy and comfortable roads. We can trust that God not only knows the way He's taking us but that His path will glorify Him. God has called us not to follow a certain path but to follow Him in faith. That is the wisdom in following the long and winding road.

Reflection Questions

1. How do long and winding roads test our faith? What practices can we do to strengthen our faith as we follow God?

2. Isaiah 55:8-9 says, "For My thoughts are not your thoughts, nor are your ways My ways," declares the LORD. "For as the heavens are higher than the earth, so are My ways higher than your ways and My thoughts than your thoughts." What does this mean, especially when God's direction doesn't make sense to us?

3. How does following God on His path instead of our own bring Him glory?

4. How is our faith today a legacy for those who come after us?

5. Joseph's bones were in the midst of the Hebrews as a reminder of God's faithfulness. Do you have any tangible reminder of God's faithfulness in your life?

Prayer

Lord, we want to follow You, but sometimes our faith falters when the road doesn't make sense. Anchor our faith when we cannot see why You're taking us on the long and winding road. May we delight to walk by faith each day, and may we leave a legacy of enduring faith that eternally impacts our children and our children's children. Not to us, O Lord, not to us, but to Your name goes all the glory for Your unfailing love and faithfulness. In Jesus' name, amen.

7

Wisdom and Influence

A few months ago, I watched a large flock of migrating robins hop around eating in the grass when they suddenly and simultaneously rose and flew off. You've probably seen ducks, gulls, and other flocking birds do this.

Scientists have long wondered how these flocks are able to coordinate such precise choreography with one fell swoop. Martin Lindstrom, in his book, *Brandwashed*, writes that birds have what scientists call a collective consciousness.[16] Termites use this "collective brain" as well.[17] Each termite mindlessly follows the behavior of another termite to build towering, complex mounds that none of them could build on their own.[18] "Only by observing and mimicking the behavior of its neighbors can a termite figure out what it should be doing," Lindstrom writes.[19]

He says humans are wired with a similar collective consciousness that causes us to "size up what those around us are doing

16.　Martin Lindstrom, *Brandwashed: Tricks Companies Use to Manipulate Our Minds and Persuade Us to Buy* (New York: Crown Business, 2011), 104.
17.　Lindstrom, *Brandwashed*, 104.
18.　Lindstrom, 104
19.　Lindstrom, 105.

and modify our own actions."[20] Research confirms over and over that we look at what others are doing to make our own decisions. In one British study, scientists told groups to walk "aimlessly around" a hall without talking to each other. They quietly gave a few people precise instructions where to walk. The result? "No matter how large or small the group, everyone in it blindly followed that handful of people who appeared to have some idea of where they were going."[21]

The researchers concluded that humans are like flocks of sheep or birds and will mindlessly follow a minority. They noted that "it takes a mere 5% of 'informed individuals' to influence the direction of a crowd of up to 200 people. The other 95% of us trail along without even being aware of it."[22]

That is the power of peer pressure. Advertisers and marketers are well acquainted with it. Lindstrom says that "we instinctively believe that others know more about what we want than we ourselves do."[23]

Peer pressure is not new to our generation. We see the power of peer pressure and worldly wisdom in a story tucked into the ancient pages of I Kings 12. It's the story of a young man who inherited the wealthiest, most successful kingdom of that day, and with his first act as king, split the kingdom in two.

This was Solomon's son, Rehoboam, grandson of King David and heir to the throne of Israel. This is the son Solomon constantly taught about wisdom throughout Proverbs. Rehoboam's first act as king split the kingdom, and his second act cost the remaining part of the kingdom all its treasure. Rehoboam is the

20. Lindstrom, 105.
21. Lindstrom, 106.
22. Lindstrom, 106
23. Lindstrom. 107.

consummate illustration of what happens when we fail to listen to godly wisdom.

We often understand the full impact of a virtue like godly wisdom when we see a life where it is completely lacking. That is what we see in the reign of Rehoboam—a man who had godly instruction from the wisest man who ever lived but gave other influences access to his heart.

Godly Counsel

The lack of godly wisdom shows up where we turn for counsel. We find the story of Rehoboam in 1 Kings 12:

> Then Rehoboam went to Shechem, because all Israel had come to Shechem to make him king. Now when Jeroboam the son of Nebat heard *of this*, he was living in Egypt (for he was still in Egypt, where he had fled from the presence of King Solomon). Then they sent and called him, and Jeroboam and all the assembly of Israel came and spoke to Rehoboam, saying, "Your father made our yoke hard; but now, lighten the hard labor imposed by your father and his heavy yoke which he put on us, and we will serve you." Then he said to them, "Depart for three days, then return to me." So the people departed. (1 Kings 12:1-5)

Foolishness refuses to listen to wisdom. Solomon, who led Israel to its Golden Age, had died, and his son Rehoboam had been crowned king. There were high hopes Rehoboam would take the kingdom to even greater heights. Even Rehoboam's name, which means "one who enlarges the people," pointed to a bigger and better future.

Not everyone, however, was quick to embrace Solomon's son as king. He was most likely crowned in Jerusalem, but the northern tribes wanted to meet him at Shechem, the ancient gathering place of the early Jews. Shechem would become the capital for a period of time for the ten northern tribes.

The Hebrews had a grievance. They wanted their taxes reduced. This is where the lack of godly wisdom first shows up. After Rehoboam was confronted with the request, he consulted with the elders who had served and counseled his father (1 Kgs. 12:6). This was a reasonable step, and Rehoboam seemed to implement the wisdom of Solomon that "where there is no guidance the people fall, but in abundance of counselors there is victory" (Prov. 11:14). But then Rehoboam made a sudden and disturbing turn.

Rehoboam "forsook the counsel of the elders which they had given him, and consulted with the young men who grew up with him and served him" (1 Kgs. 12:8). Solomon had warned about this exact kind of action. In Proverbs 12:15, Solomon stated, "The way of a fool is right in his own eyes, but a wise man is he who listens to counsel," and in Proverbs 13:20 he says, "He who walks with wise men will be wise, but the companion of fools will suffer harm."

The great theologian Paul Bear Bryant said it like this: "If you are going to be a winner you must surround yourself with winners."

It is interesting that the wisdom of the elders took only one verse. Wisdom does not always consist of long and drawn-out principles. On the other hand, the advice of Rehoboam's aristocratic peers took two verses. Foolishness speaks more than wisdom. Solomon had also warned about this, saying that the voice of a fool comes through many words (Eccles. 5:3).

We see the lack of godly wisdom in three ways in Rehoboam's response:

1. A lack of godly wisdom shows up in the absence of deportment.

When the people returned to hear Rehoboam's response, he "answered the people harshly." The reason for his harshness is found in the same verse: because "he forsook the advice of the elders." Foolishness often comes across as bullying because there is no strength in foolishness. Have you ever noticed how bullies always speak harshly, roughly, and menacingly?

Rehoboam announced that instead of reducing taxes, he would add to the people's burden: "My father made your yoke heavy, but I will add to your yoke; my father disciplined you with whips, but I will discipline you with scorpions" (1 Kgs. 12:14b). Second Chronicles 10:10 gives even more insight when Rehoboam quotes his peers, saying, "My little finger is thicker than my father's thighs" (ESV).

A lack of godly wisdom shows up in our disposition and how we speak to others.

We live in a world that bullies. As I write this, the headline in the morning news is about a fourteen-year-old girl who died by suicide after months of being bullied both at school and online. Tragically, that is a headline that we see almost on a daily basis. We live in an age when bullying people is the norm in business, school, and even the neighborhoods in which we live. It's a sign of emotional immaturity and a lack of wisdom in general in our society.

In the New Testament during the time of Christ, Rome was the big bully. For the Jews at that time, the Sadducees, Pharisees, scribes, and Herodians were also bullies. Even today as Christians, we live with those who would pressure us into one decision or another without thought of godly wisdom. Rehoboam's foolishness showed up not only in his decisions but in the way he treated his people.

2. A lack of godly wisdom reflects a lack of prayer.

What stands out in this passage is what's absent from the passage. Absolutely no one stopped to seek the LORD in prayer. Not Rehoboam, not Jeroboam, not the elders, or the young men. No one at Shechem—where the Tabernacle had been for three hundred years, where the ark had been housed, where Hebrews gathered to worship—asked to pray. No one sought the LORD and His wisdom.

Worldly wisdom is our default. If we don't stop and take the time to pray, we will never be able to operate in godly wisdom.

3. A lack of godly wisdom reflects a refusal to listen.

Rehoboam would not listen to the elders, and he also refused to listen to the people (1 Kgs. 12:15). It is obvious that he never listened to his father, Solomon, the wisest man who ever lived. Over and over, the Proverbs instruct us to listen: "My son, give attention to my wisdom, incline your ear to my understanding; that you may observe discretion and your lips may reserve knowledge" (Prov. 5:1-2).

Where we turn for counsel reveals whether we are depending on godly wisdom or rejecting it and acting foolishly in making decisions.

Disastrous Patterns

The lack of godly wisdom disastrously becomes a pattern. Forrest Gump famously said, "Stupid is as stupid does." For Rehoboam, it was not stupidity but foolishness that became a pattern in his life. Look at the consequences of Rehoboam's foolish decisions:

> When all Israel saw that the king had not listened to them, the people replied to the king, saying, "What share do we have in David? We have no inheritance in the son of Jesse; To your tents, Israel! Now look after your own house, David!"
>
> When all Israel *saw* that the king did not listen to them, the people answered the king, saying, "What portion do we have in David? *We have* no inheritance in the son of Jesse;To your tents, O Israel! Now look after your own house, David!" So Israel departed to their tents. But as for the sons of Israel who lived in the cities of Judah, Rehoboam reigned over them. Then King Rehoboam sent Adoram, who was over the forced labor, and all Israel stoned him to death. And King Rehoboam made haste to mount his chariot to flee to Jerusalem. So Israel has been in rebellion against the house of David to this day. (1 Kgs. 12:16-19 NASB)

A fool will listen only to himself. Solomon says, "The way of a fool is right in his own eyes." (Prov. 12:15). Rehoboam did not think that he was capable of making a bad decision. He foolishly sent Adoram, not as an ambassador to work through the issue with the people but as head over forced labor to decree the consequences for their insurrection. Rehoboam's decision was foolish, and the results were disastrous. Before Adoram could even speak, all Israel took him out and stoned him.

Rehoboam for his part turned tail and ran for his life, riding to Jerusalem. There he assembled 180,000 men of Judah and Benjamin to fight against the ten northern tribes. This was yet another knee-jerk, foolish decision. Only by God's intervention speaking through the prophet Shemaiah did they avoid a civil war. God told Rehoboam he was not to go up and fight against his relatives but that every man was to return to his house (1 Kgs. 12:24).

While Rehoboam did what the LORD commanded in this instance, it was isolated obedience. One act of obedience in a difficult situation does not make a disciple of godly wisdom. It is the consistent godly wisdom in decisions over the course of our lives that makes a difference. Rehoboam never learned this. Foolishness and wickedness became a disastrous pattern in his life. It was during Rehoboam's reign that Judah turned to all kinds of detestable idolatry. Sadly, Solomon had warned about this as well: "Doing wickedness is like sport to a fool" (Prov. 10:23).

While Judah was wrapped up in idolatry, Shishak, king of Egypt, invaded the land. When he entered Jerusalem, he either took or was given the treasures of the temple, including the marvelous golden shields that Solomon had made during the height of his reign.

These golden shields had been brought out on special occasions. The king's guard would form a double line, each holding a golden shield, and the king would walk through with the eastern sun splashing down against them. By all accounts, it was a dazzling, blinding, stunningly impressive ceremony.

But under Rehoboam's reign, the Egyptian king took those shields to Egypt as a prize. Foolishly and egotistically, Rehoboam would not give up the ceremony of walking through the streets of Jerusalem up to the magnificent temple his father had built, and he had shields of bronze made in their place.

Can you imagine the scene when Rehoboam appeared in the streets of Jerusalem? He was headed up to the temple, walking between young, well-trained, elite forces. But they carried a poor substitute for gold shields. No gleaming in the sun; no dazzling, spectacular, shimmering shields of gold. Instead, they held the dull, lackluster, "brown" of bronze. If anything, it was a sign that the glory of God no longer hovered over the holy city. They had profaned the city, and Rehoboam, in his foolishness, had paved the way for the treasure that had been left in his care to be captured by the pure pagans.

This is not just an ancient story of foolishness. The story of Rehoboam holds three critical principles for us today as we seek to make godly decisions in our own lives:

1. Be very discerning about whom you allow to walk into your home.

We cannot help who crosses our path, but we can be discerning about who walks into our home. Scripture tells us the young men who counseled Rehoboam also served him. They were there in his home, in his palace, with him at meals and events. They told him what he wanted to hear, which stoked his ego but constantly filled his ear with ungodly wisdom.

2. Beware of whom you let speak into your thoughts.

Whoever gets hold of our attention will speak into our thoughts. These young men were untested and unproven. They were not like the elders who had wisely served Solomon for years. Their counsel had been tried and found true. Not so with these peers, pressuring Rehoboam to listen to them perhaps out of their own ego so they could claim they had influenced the king.

3. Be careful whom you allow to have your heart.

So often, brilliant men will give their hearts to someone who so captivates them that their normally good judgment in decisions becomes tainted by desire, overshadowed by emotion, and infected by passions. They stop making good decisions. Sometimes they stop making decisions at all, handing off the decision-making process to whomever has their heart.

Bill O'Reilly, in his fascinating book *Killing the Legends,* recounts the life and death of three celebrated men who had extraordinary talent and ability—Elvis Presley, John Lennon, and Muhammad Ali. These three men were amazingly successful in their professions. But tragically, each one ended up influenced by a major personality whom they let walk into their homes, speak into their thoughts, and capture their hearts to the degree that all three ended up making disastrous decisions over their lives.

Godly wisdom means guarding who has access to our heart. We cannot give in to the peer pressure surrounding us. As I heard my mother say a thousand times, "Do not be deceived: Bad company corrupts good morals" (1 Cor. 15:33).

Reflection Questions

1. What are the biggest areas in which you feel peer pressure in your life?

2. Where is the first place you tend to go for counsel in a situation? Do you go to someone who will tell you what you want to hear? What characteristics help you find someone you can trust for godly counsel?

3. What part does prayer play in seeking godly counsel?

4. Whom are you allowing to walk into your home? Whom are you allowing to speak into your thoughts? Whom are you allowing to have your heart?

5. What does 1 Corinthians 15:33 mean when it says, "Do not be deceived: Bad company corrupts good morals?"

Prayer

God, I ask Your forgiveness for the times I haven't sought Your counsel, I haven't prayed over a decision, and I've given into ungodly peer pressure. I desperately need Your wisdom for my relationships, my parenting, my work, my home, my finances, my walk with You. Without You, I can do nothing. Help me discern any person or thing speaking into my life that is not aligned with Your Word. Will You give me godly friendships and godly mentors who will feed me truth? Guard my heart from anything that would take me from You. In Jesus' name, amen.

Wisdom: From Panic to Praise

Nothing ever passes into our life that does not first come under the vigilant eye of God the Father, through the nail-scarred hands of Jesus, and past the sentinel safeguard of the Holy Spirit.

When we last saw the Hebrews, they were poised on the banks of the Red Sea as sitting ducks. They were bait in a trap for Pharaoh. They found themselves with an insurmountable obstacle before them, an unconquerable army behind them, and an un-navigable wilderness on each side of them. It was as if following God had placed them in a trap with no escape. And their response was to panic.

Panic drains the blood from our brain, causes our heart to race, and makes our stomach flip. In that state, we revert to doing whatever fear dictates. The Hebrews panicked because of their focus on Pharaoh and the Egyptian army. Exodus 14:10 says, "As Pharaoh drew near, the sons of Israel looked, and behold, the Egyptians were marching after them, and they became very frightened." We saw that Moses told them to stop it by using a double negative, the strongest expression in Hebrew (Exod. 14:13). Moses redirected their attention to the LORD and what the LORD was about to do. Moses likely motioned toward the cloud of God's presence, which was right before them.

Then the LORD asked Moses, "Why are you crying out to Me?" (Exod. 14:15). But Hebrews tells us that Moses walked out of Egypt in bold faith: "By faith, [Moses] left Egypt, not fearing the wrath of the king; for he endured, as seeing Him who is unseen" (Heb. 11:27).

So why did the LORD ask Moses, "Why are you crying to Me?" It was the Hebrews who were crying out, not Moses. However, when God spoke to Moses, He accredited to Moses the cries of the people. That is, God credited to Moses the cries of the nation, as if Moses were the one crying out. This is a picture of the coming Christ, to whom was imputed our sin, as if He were the one who sinned.

God spoke and told the Hebrews to move forward (Exod. 14:15). This is so important. Before God ever instructed Moses what to do and before He ever opened the path through the Red Sea, He instructed the Hebrews to move forward. We are to walk into insurmountable obstacles trusting God. The question becomes, How do we do that? How do we get our eyes off what is causing the panic and walk into the insurmountable?

Worship. This entire section in Exodus is wrapped by two great worship experiences. The first is the Passover, which celebrated salvation by the blood of a lamb. The other is on the other side of the Red Sea when God delivered the Hebrews. Let's look at two guiding principles that can help us go from panic to praise.

Worship and Obedience

Worship grows out of obedience. When panic sets in, it's like gangrene—it will eat up all that is good and kill all that is healthy if we are not careful. Obedience pulls us out of panic.

In Exodus 14:15-16, we find three ways God guides us:

1. God will guide out of direction.

The casualty in panic is direction. When we panic, we turn in every direction and have no clue where to go. This was the state of the Hebrews, hemmed in on every side. But God gave them clear direction so that they didn't even have to think. He said to move forward. Forward meant moving toward the insurmountable obstacle, the Red Sea.

But note what God said next: "The sons of Israel shall go through the midst of the sea" (Exod. 14:16). Now, that may not seem any easier, but it certainly provided clarity. When we choose to obey God, He will give us a clear direction even though the way looks impossible. The only way for the people of God to move is forward.

The first time General Ulysses Grant met General Robert E. Lee in battle, it was hell. It was the Battle of the Wilderness in May of 1864. There was a severe drought, and during the battle, the wilderness literally caught on fire. Most men died from being burned alive. The Union lost seventeen thousand men, and the Confederacy lost seven thousand. The Union withdrew from the horror, and as they did, it started to rain. The Union forces expected to retreat back across the Virginia line to the North, but the new Union general would never retreat. In the night and in the rain as the Union forces came to the crossroads, they found a muddy, wet, unkempt Grant smoking a cigar, pointing them back to the South.

Often, God will block every other route of retreat and point us to move forward toward what seems to be impossible.

2. *God will guide with protection.*

> The angel of God, who had been going before the camp of Israel, moved and went behind them; and the pillar of cloud moved from before them and stood behind them. So it came between the camp of Egypt and the camp of Israel; and there was the cloud along with the darkness, yet it gave light at night. Thus the one did not come near the other all night. (Exod. 14:19-20)

The angel of the LORD that had been going before the Hebrews moved and went behind them, coming between them and the Egyptians. While it appears from the text that the cloud brought complete darkness, the word in Hebrew means obscurity. For the Hebrews, however, there was light through the night.

God has no problem keeping us separated from that which will hurt us, whoever our enemy might be. When Moses stretched out his hand over the sea, God caused a strong east wind to blow and separate the sea. The Song of Moses in chapter 15 tells us the wind was a blast of air from the nostrils of God (Exod. 15:8). Whether this is poetic or literal, it demonstrates that separating the sea was so easy for God that it was like exhaling. The sea stood up on both sides and congealed or thickened, as it means in Hebrew (Exod. 15:8). It was as if they were walking through the glass tunnel in the Atlanta Aquarium.

The Hebrews walked across that entire sea on dry ground. They didn't have to slog their way through mud. It was as dry as the desert floor. They were protected from the army behind, from the water to each side, and from the miry mud below. That is how God guides with protection.

3. God will guide to completion.

> At the morning watch, the LORD looked down on the army of the Egyptians through the pillar of fire and cloud and brought the army of the Egyptians into confusion. (Exod. 14:24)

God saw the Egyptians, and He threw confusion into the midst of their plans: "He caused their chariot wheels to swerve, and He made them drive with difficulty; so the Egyptians said, 'Let us flee from Israel, for the LORD is fighting for them against the Egyptians'" (Exod. 14:25). It's almost comical that the Egyptians now refered to themselves in the third person, as if they no longer wanted to be the Egyptians!

The Hebrews stood on the banks of the other side of the Red Sea watching all of this chaos take place. They watched the sea engulf and drown the Egyptian army. While it must have been emotional for them, they needed to see this to know that the looming threat that had caused them so much anguish was no more.

We need the same thing. We need to know that what God saved us from will never separate us from Him again. When God saved us, He saved us spiritually, physically, emotionally, and mentally. In every way we could be saved, we have been saved, if we have come to Jesus Christ.

Now, some of those Hebrews walked through the sea with confidence, excitement, and boldness. Others walked through with trembling, terrified that the walls of water could come crashing down on them. Regardless of whether their faith was strong or weak, they were all saved. It wasn't the quality of their faith or even the quantity of their faith, but the object of their faith that saved them.

Out of their obedience, they experienced God's salvation. And interestingly, once they started moving forward, their grumbling stopped, panic subsided, and fear dissipated. What came next was an outburst of worship.

Worship and Thanksgiving

Worship expresses itself in thanksgiving. The first song recorded in all the Word of God happens on the banks of the Red Sea (Exod. 15). Worship springs from a heart of thanksgiving. Job tells us the morning stars sang together and the sons of God shouted for joy at creation (Job 38:7). Deborah sang when Israel defeated Jabin and Sisera. David sang when God delivered him from his enemies. The people of God sing out of a heart of worship that expresses itself in thanksgiving.

When we come into the church sanctuary and begin services with a song of praise and thanksgiving, it's not to get us in a mood, pump us up, or set an atmosphere. We sing when we gather out of hearts that overflow with thanksgiving. This doesn't happen anywhere else all week. It is different from singing at home or singing with a school choir, and it's different from the excitement that comes at a stadium at a sporting event. When we gather as believers, we are part of the choir of God. That's what Colossians 3:16 tells us:

> Let the word of Christ richly dwell within you, with all wisdom teaching and admonishing one another with psalms *and* hymns *and* spiritual songs, singing with thankfulness in your hearts to God.

We see three elements in the Hebrews' worship. First, no one taught them how to sing. When we have a thankful heart, we just do it. Second, no one taught them what to sing. They knew what to sing. Third, no one taught them how to sing together. When a group of people gather in community, they know from whom all their blessings flow. There's no need to teach them how to sing together. They just do it.

The theme of this song was not about Moses or how they felt, like so many contemporary songs that focus on man and our emotions. This was a song about the LORD and His glory. We see that in three ways:

1. Celebration of who God is

The proper name LORD, or Yahweh, is used eleven times in their song. Other personal pronouns referring to Him are used about thirty times. This song is about Him and to Him. We see this all throughout: He is highly exalted (Exod. 15:1), He is majestic (Exod. 15:6), He is holiness, and He is awesome (Exod. 15:11).

The words of Exodus 15:11 are a great place to start with worship: "Who is like You among the gods, O LORD? Who is like You, majestic in holiness, awesome in praises, working wonders?"

2. Thanksgiving for what God has done

The most famous expression from this song is, "The horse and its rider He has thrown into the sea." Moses and the men sang it, and then Miriam sang it. Their song details God's salvation, saying they sank like a stone (Exod. 15:5), sank like lead (Exod. 15:10), and that God completely shattered the enemy (Exod. 15:6). This defeat was so thorough that Egypt didn't attack Israel again until the days of Solomon, roughly five hundred years later. When God saves, He does it like no one else.

3. *Expectation of salvation*

In Revelation 15:1-3, we find seven angels with seven plagues to be poured out on the earth. Before the throne was a sweeping sea of glass and fire. Fire indicates the judgment of God, and chapter 15 is in fact about the final judgments of God on this world. Standing before the throne were those who were victorious over the beast.

These had come out of the great tribulation with their testimonies intact. They made it through the most horrible time on earth for Christians. As they entered heaven, what were they doing?

They were singing the Song of Moses (Rev. 15:3). It spoke of the ultimate victory of God and His people. Out of this great tribulation, these Christians were obedient, they followed the LORD, and that led them to worship.

Nearly every morning, I get up and look for the latest on the war in Ukraine. I've taken three mission trips there, my wife has taken four, and we took our children with us on most of those trips. We saw thousands come to Christ. We visited hospitals, schools, and orphanages. We preached on street corners and handed out hundreds of thousands of Bibles. We planted churches and financially helped to build others.

In the midst of this war, the Ukrainian Christians have continued to gather for worship. They call their praise songs "weapons of warfare."

One church leader told *Christianity Today*, "Our minds fail to understand: How is this possible in this day and age? God allowed this to happen, and we do not know why. But we know

God is sovereign, and he is on his throne. There are people who think if they kill someone it will accomplish a goal." A worship leader said, "Our hope is in the LORD, the one who holds things together. No matter how things fall apart, the LORD created this world, and he holds things in his hands." He played music and led worship in tears. But he also told his church family, "Even if a nuclear attack happens, the hope we have is we go home. And we will be together with Jesus, the one we know will help us."[24]

Remember that nothing ever passes into our life but that it does not first come under the vigilant eye of God the Father, through the nail-scarred hands of Jesus, and past the sentinel safeguard of the Holy Spirit. Instead of giving into panic when we face insurmountable obstacles, wisdom allows us, like these Ukrainian Christians, to redirect our focus to God and turn worry into worship.

Reflection Questions

1. How do we move forward to follow God when an obstacle in front of us is insurmountable? What does that look like practically?

2. How does worship help us when we are tempted to panic because of our circumstances?

3. How is worship an act of obedience?

4. Have you seen God guide you with protection? Describe how God protected you.

5. How is worship tied to thanksgiving?

24. Emily Belz, "Ukrainian American Churches Deploy Praise as a Weapon," *Christianity Today*, February 28, 2022.

Prayer

O LORD, who is like You among the gods? Who is like You, majestic in holiness, awesome in praises, working wonders? Oh God, You are my God. Thank You for guiding me, for protecting me, for going before me, and for saving me. Thank You for the faithful ways You care for me and have met my needs. Thank You for waking me in the morning with purpose and keeping me through the watches of the night. Thank You for Your sustaining grace. Because Your love is better than life, my lips will glorify You. I will praise You as long as I live. In Jesus' name, amen.

Epilogue
Clarity in Crisis

In battle, it is said that soldiers are often confused as to the direction of the enemy. The chaos of crisis makes it hard to know which direction to move. It must have been that way for the disciples that night out on the Sea of Galilee when they were caught in a storm that spun into a crisis. The gospel writers tell us that the disciples were in the darkest part of the night, in the deepest part of the sea, exhausted from trying to control the little boat in the storm that swirled around them. However, it was then that the Lord Jesus came walking to them on the very waves of their crisis.

Christ always meets you in your crisis. That is where I found myself in the weeks before I made the crucial decision to trust God, to believe that He had a ministry somewhere for me. Deb and I had gone with Bob and Pam Tebow to the jungles of the Philippines to train pastors. It was the hardest week working I can ever remember. Bob had me teaching and preaching from eight o'clock in the morning to around nine o'clock at night. There were breaks for meals and a little sleep. In the midst of the chaos that swirled around me, I threw myself into pouring into the lives of men who had little education, little in the way of the comforts of life that I knew and enjoyed. It was exactly what God had in mind for us. When I put myself aside, and emptied myself into the lives of others, the wisdom of God began to blow away the brain fog and spiritual fatigue and gave me hope of a well-defined direction.

To walk away from what I had always believed was God's place for me until retirement or He called me home, to leave our dream home and the place where our children and grandchildren lived, seemed like a burden too heavy to bear. However, God's wisdom made the decision clear. When the direction was clear, the decision was easy, and the pieces of life and ministry fell into place. Unknown to me, God's wisdom was directing me to a door God was opening. I simply had to be obedient to follow.

All along I had prayed at least once or twice a day the words of Psalm 118:5-9:

> From my distress I called upon the Lord;
> The Lord answered me and set me in a large place.
> The Lord is for me; I will not fear;
> What can man do to me?
> The Lord is for me among those who help me;
> Therefore I will look with satisfaction on those who hate me.
> It is better to take refuge in the Lord
> Than to trust in man.
> It is better to take refuge in the Lord
> Than to trust in princes.

God did just as He said and as I had prayed. He gave me a broad place. That's an interesting Hebraism. It means a place where there is no constriction, no vise that squeezes the breath out of you. It's a place that is wide open, airy, and free. Godly wisdom led me to a people who longed for me as much as I longed for them. A place that loves the preaching and teaching of the word of God. A place where they long to be led, long to be a part, long to be in fellowship and community together. It was as if the Lord dropped me at the wedding feast of Cana of Galilee, and said, "I have saved the best for last for you."

Toward the end of the fascinating story of Joseph, his brothers who had betrayed him, mistreated him, ostracized, and demeaned him, stand face to face with him once again. Joseph states that all that they had done to him they intended for evil. However, God used it all for good. See Genesis 50:20:

> As for you, you meant evil against me,
> but God meant it for good . . .

That was the miracle of Godly wisdom in Joseph's life. There is evidence of the work of the wisdom of God in Joseph's life. He calls his brothers together and he tells them that he is about to die, but then he immediately states in Genesis 50:24:

> . . . but God will surely take care of you and bring you up from this land to the land which He promised on oath to Abraham, to Isaac and to Jacob.

A second time Joseph says that in Genesis 50:25. The amazing thing is how Joseph still cares for those who so cruelly mistreated him. In a moment when he could have legitimately been thinking of himself, he thought of what was best for them. When I laid down the ministry that I am convinced God led me to and that He had laid on me, I was doing what I believed was best for them. Joseph was ministering to them when they should have been ministering to him. The wisdom of God leaves no room and no necessity for acrimony, pettiness, or resentment. It does bring His peace in the midst of the chaos of crisis. It does bring the understanding that what man intended for evil, God uses for good.

And we know that God causes all things to work together for good to those who love God, to those who are called according to His purpose. (Romans 8:28)

God Cares for You

SCAN HERE to learn more about Invite Press, a premier publishing imprint created to invite people to a deeper faith and living relationship with Jesus Christ.

Printed in the USA
CPSIA information can be obtained
at www.ICGtesting.com
CBHW041304170124
3209CB00008B/12